Dying can seriously
damage your health

Dying can seriously damage your health

*Your Guide to the weird world
of Health and Safety*

researched and written by Maurice Fells
with commentaries by Lesley Turney

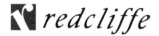 *redcliffe*

First published in 2009 by Redcliffe Press Ltd.,
81g Pembroke Road, Bristol BS8 3EA
www.redcliffepress.co.uk
info@redcliffepress.co.uk

© Maurice Fells and Lesley Turney
© this collection Redcliffe Press Ltd

ISBN 978-1-906593-32-2

British Library Cataloguing-in-Publication Data:
A catalogue record for this book is available from the British Library.

Cover design by Dan Bramall and Simon Bishop,
typesetting by Harper Phototypesetters Ltd
and printed by HSW Print, Tonypandy, Rhondda

Contents

Publishers' note *6*
Safety regulations, political correctness
and the compensation culture 7

School is a dangerous place *10*
'Nanny State' edicts *32*
The Great – and risky – Outdoors *38*
Food isn't always good for you *50*
Mind your language *61*
We're only doing it for your sake …
to avoid a compensation claim *82*
The whackiest insurance claims *102*
In the Courts *111*
No Christmas joy *114*
Would you believe it? *125*
Health and Safety hit back *144*

Stop Press *150*

Publishers' Note

We have not fabricated any of these stories. All have appeared in the national or local media. However, we cannot check the authenticity of all of them, nor the accuracy of the words attributed to the persons involved. Some may have been misquoted; others may have come to regret words spoken in haste. Taking the view that the stories − not the personalities − and the cultures they highlight are what's important, in many cases we have opted for anonymity, or changed names, for the 'innocent' parties. Where people were speaking officially, we have assumed that they stand by their statements and will not be embarrassed by their repetition.

Safety regulations, political correctness and the compensation culture

It started, as these things often do, in a pub. A few of us were enjoying a drink and putting the world to rights when the conversation turned to the latest in a seemingly endless stream of stories about health and safety edicts. On this occasion, a certain city council had told tenants living in flats and high-rise blocks that 'hazardous doormats' constituted a tripping danger, and were to be removed forthwith.

We conducted a brief and entirely unscientific survey amongst ourselves, and discovered that nobody had ever had an actual close encounter with a dangerous doormat; all the ones we knew were fairly benign objects. So we turned our attention to similar examples of cases we'd heard, or read of where guidelines had been issued to protect us from dangers we often didn't even know we faced. On further investigation, some of these turned out to be genuine, others mythical. For instance, there were the schoolchildren forbidden from using the inside tubes of toilet rolls or empty egg boxes in their craft projects in case they harboured germs. Others had, allegedly, been told they had to wear safety goggles if they wanted to play conkers at school. Pancake races had been banned because of the potential risks to life and limb posed by over-excited adults wielding heavy pans – not to mention the hygiene issues associated with the accidental dropping of tossed batter. Last, but far from least, there was the apocryphal regulation that said from now on, trapeze artists had to wear hard hats to protect their heads if they fell from a great height. Absolute nonsense, we are assured by the Health & Safety Executive. As ever, elements in the nation's media don't allow the facts to get in the way of a good story; any more than we do, in repeating them here.

With so much material to hand, it seemed a good idea to put together a book of some of the best – or most entertaining – health and safety stories of the past few years. For good measure, we've also thrown in a few examples of preposterous insurance claims and political correctness, if not actually gone mad, then at least veering towards the slightly eccentric.

This book is intended to be a bit of fun. We leave others – and there are such organisations – to do the campaigning. For our part, we don't doubt that the people responsible for looking after our best interests do genuinely have our best interests at heart, and there's usually a good reason for new regulations. But it's hard to believe that young children's futures could be blighted because they don't succeed in the school egg-and-spoon race, or that a two-week-old baby's dignity is harmed by being coo-ed at by doting family and friends. We question, too, the need for 'falls prevention fitness advisers' and wonder just who benefits from Christmas carols being theologically-modified and politically-corrected.

But we have no high horses to mount, no axes to grind and no grudges to bear. We simply want to share the innocent pleasure of smiling at some of the idiocies of modern life in Britain. In most cases we've given the sources for stories that have already appeared in the national press, and we haven't flinched from repeating good tales that turned out to have been wildly exaggerated by an over-enthusiastic British media, or in some cases, entirely fictitious. It is interesting to note that some newspapers seem to choose not to report these stories, while others 'go to town' in exposing absurdities. Perhaps it's a political thing.

So please enjoy these offerings, don't take them too seriously, have a chuckle, but don't laugh too energetically – we don't want to be sued by readers with cracked ribs.

School is a dangerous place

Schools have always been dangerous places. In the not-so-very-distant past, children were regularly beaten with canes, slippers or similar objects designed to inflict maximum pain in short, sharp shocks. Every school pupil worth his or her salt developed lightning-fast reflexes in order to avoid being hit on the head by sticks of chalk or blackboard rubbers thrown by irascible teachers. These dangers were once not only legal, they were deemed to be character-building, and positively good for us. One friend's science teacher was nicknamed 'Bonk' because he would patrol the classroom aisles, for no apparent reason thumping pupils on the head with clenched fist. And in reality how many millions of unsporty children have been mentally scarred, over the years, by being bullied into climbing ropes (and let's be honest, how many of us have ever needed that skill in our adult lives?), or running for miles in the rain across country, gasping asthmatically at every step, or suffering countless injuries on the sports fields? All this without even touching on the myriad perils of the playground.

Those were what some people still refer to as 'the good old days' when children knew their place and physical, emotional and verbal abuse were nothing more than tools for maintaining order in the classroom.

That doesn't happen any more. It's not allowed. But there are still sinister forces at work.... These days, others dangers have been brought to light – dangers most of us weren't even aware of, dangers so perilous that countless bans have been introduced up and down the country in order to protect our youth from things like... balloons, snow and paper aeroplanes.

We may roll our eyes and wonder what the world's coming to, but sadly these bans have all been introduced to protect school staff, and ultimately us, the taxpayers, from compensation claims. Believe it or not, a pupil whose finger was hit by a cricket ball recently was awarded £5,000 and the one who was injured while breaking into school at night time, in the dark, found himself £6,000 better off. You couldn't make it up! Old-timers shake their heads in disbelief to see 10-year-old boys wearing cricket helmets, when the fastest young bowler would struggle to get the ball to bounce waist-high, let alone threaten the batsman's head. All down to fear – not on the child's part, nor of his being hurt, but his parents bringing a law suit against the school or the hapless bowler.

The perils of school are many and varied. Most parents will have put on a brave face while enduring a number of school concerts so I suppose we ought to spare a thought for the long-suffering music teachers....

Music teachers ordered to wear earmuffs

[*Daily Mail January 21 2009*]

School music teachers have been warned to wear earmuffs or stand behind noise screens to protect their hearing. This is because beginners tend to blast away much louder than professionals.

The most potentially deafening instrument is the cornet, with just one honk being enough to cause permanent ear damage. Standing next to a school band is even more dangerous, warns the Health and Safety Executive.

And while we're on the subject of noise....

Teachers want to ban school bells, after deeming them a health hazard

Members of the Scottish Secondary Teachers' Association have complained that the school bell system – used to mark breaks between classes – is too noisy. They claim that regular exposure to these bells, throughout the school week, can cause irreversible damage to hearing in the long-term. But education activists have branded the plans 'health and safety gone mad'. The teachers are proposing a four-bell system that will ring periodically, as opposed to the traditional single bell that rings continuously.

Under the weather

The weather is a constant source of worry – not to say obsession – to most people in the UK, but this

anxiety is much, much worse for those in charge of the health and well-being of the nation's under-11s. And despite the relative paucity of good weather in this country, it's the sun that causes the most problems for the authorities.

'Over-sunny weather' is close to the top of the long list of threats to our children. During the last heat-wave, Derby City Council told its teachers it might be best to postpone out-of-school trips until the weather cooled, because of fears the children might develop skin cancer if they spent too long outdoors.

The council's circular advised: 'Try to plan external activities – short-duration trips, external lessons, sports days – for times when the sun is likely to be at its lowest.' But it didn't go so far as to recommend late-night outings, when there would have been no risk at all of sun-stroke or cancer.

It also suggested keeping a supply of sunscreen to hand, not cream but the spray variety because it is recommended adults avoid the potential morally dangerous physical contact necessary to rub cream onto the pupils' skins.

Hurt feelings...
B dropped from school class name
[*BBC News June 5 2006*]
A school has changed the names of its primary one classes after complaints that they left some children feeling inferior.

Bonnyrigg Primary School, Scotland, had called its classes 1a and 1b but some parents of children in 1b said it left the youngsters feeling second best. The classes will now be known as 1ar and 1ap, incorporating teachers' surnames in the new titles.

One Midlothian parent dubbed the move 'political correctness gone mad'. The man said he was surprised when he read about the change in a school newsletter. He told the BBC Scotland news website: 'This shows how far political correctness has gone in Scotland.

'I thought this policy was simply astounding. I have to admit that I am surprised that the headmistress has bowed to, and thereby endorsed, this.'

Eleanor Coner, Scottish Parent Teacher Council information officer, said she was 'flabbergasted' by the school's decision to rename its classes. She said: 'There is a long history of giving classes names and therefore it seems logical to go with the start of the alphabet.

'These parents need not be so sensitive and should think whether it is not their actions which are highlighting this inferior idea surrounding class names.

'It all sounds a bit silly to me and is on a par with the situation which brought us the changed nursery rhyme name of "Ba Ba Rainbow Sheep".

'These parents need to get a grip, it's a ridiculous request, which has left me flabbergasted.'

Councillor Peter Boyes, Midlothian Council cabinet member for education and lifelong learning said: 'The school was approached by some parents of primary one pupils last year who expressed some concern about the use of primary '1a' and '1b' in case 'b' was perceived as being second to 'a'.

'This is clearly not the case in the school where the two-stream, primary one classes are allocated by date of birth.

'However the headteacher took the pragmatic step of renaming the classes '1ar' and '1ap', as the new class identifiers, where 'r' and 'p' are the initials of the class teacher's surname. This practice is used elsewhere in primary schools and is not unique to Bonnyrigg Primary.'

Paper planes can be lethal

Staff at Bishops Down Primary School in Tunbridge Wells, Kent, have introduced a ban on pupils throwing paper planes at each other.

The youngsters are still allowed to make the darts but are being supervised to ensure they only launch them at the special targets which have been set up instead, which of course takes all the fun out of it.

In our day, among milder classroom japes like balancing a book on top of a partly open door to fall on an entering teacher's head, propelling ink pellets around the classroom was a messy past-time to be generally deplored. We remember one especially nasty trick we used to get up to at school. It involved a home-made catapult with a flat piece of wood, tightly bound to a matchbox by an elastic band. A 'live' match would then be released by levering back the strip of wood, the match igniting as it was gradually released and then propelled at high speed towards its victim. Now *that* ought to be banned!

School ties must be loosened

At least ten schools a week are adopting clip-on ties amid fears that conventional knots pose an injury risk, according to a report in the *Daily Telegraph* in May 2009. Concerns have been raised about children pulling them too tight and getting them caught in machinery. Headteachers also claim they look scruffy when pupils wear wide knots or short tails as part of fashion crazes.

Research by the Schoolwear Association, which represents uniform manufacturers, said there had been a rising demand for 'safer' ties this year

Two too-blondes banned by school

[*Western Daily Press January 23 2009*]

Two girls have been banned from school for being too blonde. Raegan B and another pupil, both 16, were told not to return to school until they had dyed their bleached locks a 'natural colour'.

Ms B said she was threatened with exclusion by the head of her school in Gloucestershire. She has so far refused to change. The rules applied to all, said the head.

Sports Days and Playground Games

Really rough games, like the infamous British Bulldog, have been banned from school playgrounds for many years now, but the truth is many children *like* games which have that slight element of danger. It's the risk that adds all the excitement and helps

them learn how far they can reasonably go before they get hurt. If you stop them playing one particular game, it's more than likely they'll invent something along the same lines to compensate. This leads to more bans and so on *ad infinitum*. Another regrettable trend is the fear of accidental injury during physical activities shifting from the playground to the sports field. There have been increasing reports of schools outlawing fun activities, just in case something awful goes wrong, even when nothing awful has ever gone wrong in the history of education.

Finally, some schools are now stopping sports days to spare the feelings of the losers. Anyone who's ever been the last to be picked for a team at school will sympathise. The effort of trying to look as if you don't care when really you want the ground to swallow you up is something those of us who've been through it will never forget. And being picked on by sports teachers who never understood that some of us just couldn't hit/catch/throw a ball no matter how hard we tried. But those who aren't good at sport tend to be good at other things, and, frankly, once you've survived the humiliation of sports days at school, nothing in your adult life is ever likely to be quite so bad ... so maybe coping with losing is a lesson best learned young.

Ban on playground contact

[*BBC News February 12 2007*]

A Lincolnshire school has banned physical playground games because pupils were copying violent computer games, making playtime too rough.

The ban was introduced at St. John's Primary at Bracebridge Heath near Lincoln.

The ban involves contact playground games like tag and kiss chase. Sports like football or cricket are not part of the ban.

The school said it had introduced non-physical games chosen by pupils.

Headteacher Susan Tuck said: 'The children are watching television, they're watching films and they're playing computer games, very often it's the violent element of that they are seeing and hearing.

'That's what they're going to come on to our playground to play, we want to change that picture.'

Lincolnshire Education Authority said it was up to individual schools to decide what they allowed at playtime.

But Joe F, the play development officer at The Cheeky Monkey's after-school club in Bulwell, Nottinghamshire, said contact games should be encouraged. All children love to play games, lots of physical running around, having a laugh, falling over.

'Sometimes children do have accidents, that's part and parcel of growing up and achieving.'

Injury fears stop rounders match

[*BBC News July 2005*]

A school has stopped a staff-against-pupils rounders game, because of fears that kids could get hurt.

The annual rounders match at Hollybrook Junior School had been going for 30 years, but worries the adults' size could hurt kids put a stop to the game.

Headteacher Simon Watkins defended the ban, even though the school accident book revealed more staff were getting hurt in the game than children!

And he pointed out that the school still offered a wide range of sports.

The headteacher added that lots of schools had dropped similar staff-against-pupils events.

But some parents of children at the school think the ban is batty. One told the *Daily Express* newspaper: 'Not to give pupils the chance to take part in a tradition that has been going so long is ridiculous.'

Sports day ban on parents 'to spare the losers'

[*Daily Telegraph June 16 2003*]

A primary school has banned parents from attending its annual sports day, with egg-and-spoon and obstacle races, to spare the children from embarrassment if they do not win.

Instead, a non-competitive sports day will be held behind closed doors.

The head said in a letter to parents: 'Taking part in traditional races can be difficult and often embarrassing for many children, which is why we envisage a different outdoor activity event that will suit all children.'

The move has infuriated many parents. Rob B, 43 years old, who has two sons at the school, said: 'It is political correctness gone mad. They are trying to solve a problem that does not exist.

'Children do not become scarred for life if they lose the egg-and-spoon race. They all love being in the races and they love the fact that their parents are there to cheer them on.' Mr B, who runs an export company, said that he and other parents had written to the school in protest, but he had yet to receive a reply.

Mrs W, the head, said she had made her decision after talks with parents, children, teachers and governors. 'We want to ensure that all our children take part and enjoy the experience. We expect to be able to involve parents next year.'

Birmingham education authority said: 'Each school decides the most appropriate way to arrange activities in consultation with staff and governors and looking at the needs of all the pupils.'

Sack race 'health risk'
[*The Times July 14 2008*]
The sack race and three-legged race have been banned from a school sports day because the children might fall over and hurt themselves.

Parents and campaigners described the move as 'completely over the top'.

Teachers at John F. Kennedy Primary School in Washington dropped the events after discussions with Beamish Open Air Museum where the Edwardian-themed sports day is being held.

About 375 children are dressing up in period costume for the event. Running, hopping and throwing table-tennis balls into buckets will be allowed. At least until someone suggests ways in which they could be dangerous.

This school went one step further....

Sports day banned as too competitive
[*Metro July 14 2006*]
'Threatening' events such as the sack race and the egg-and-spoon have been banned by a primary school in Sunderland in favour of a fitness and fun day.

'Some children hate sports days and dread it,' said the headteacher. 'This means that threat isn't hanging over them.' Whatever happened, we wonder, to the idea that learning to lose graciously helped children develop mature attitudes in adult life.

Killer cakes
Parents at a Wiltshire primary school have been told that home-made butterfly buns and chocolate cakes would no longer be welcome at fundraising events, because of potential insurance claims over anything not bought at a shop.

The ban also prevented pupils bringing their own cakes from home to share on birthdays. The reaction to Wiltshire

County Council's initiative was furious. A Tory councillor, John Thompson, described the letter from the headteacher as preposterous.

'The world is full of people blowing one another up and we're worried about killer cream cakes,' he said. 'Soon we'll be wrapping our children up in cotton wool.'

The county council said a circular had only contained 'guidelines' and Crudwell was the only school so far to ban home-made fare. 'Schools should avoid selling home-made products,' a spokesman said, 'as they cannot be completely sure about the conditions in which the food items have been stored or prepared.

'Such foods include cream or other dairy products, mayonnaise, eggs, fish and meat. The person who provides the food, the school or the county council could be held liable if somebody did become ill.'

Over in Wales, parents at a primary school have been warned that their home-made Christmas cakes could be a health and safety hazard.

A headteacher has banned home-cooked mince pies and other seasonal fayre from being sold at the annual Christmas fête for fear a child could have an allergic reaction to the ingredients. But the decision has upset some parents, who argue home-cooked food is often the healthier option.

Neil Davies, the headteacher at a junior school near Porthcawl, said: 'I have got to guarantee the health and safety of the pupils. I'm not doing it to upset anybody.'

However, Peter Foley, of Bridgend County Council, said 'Children are going to be gorging themselves on home-made products in the Christmas season and I see no harm in them being on sale.'

Conkers

Ahhh… what else summons up such a feeling of contented nostalgia in the heart of the grown-up English man and woman as the humble conker! Remember kicking around in the autumn leaves in the search for the bounty? Hoping you'd spot one before your brother? The exquisite delight of those blissfully shiny, polished brown nuts nestling in their soft shells, the joy of finding particularly big or beautiful ones, the excitement of soaking them in vinegar, or drying them in the oven, before skewering a hole through the middle and preparing the conker for battle! Conkers represent everything that's good, and simple and natural about being a child.

Not any more they don't.

Oh no! More than perhaps anything else, conkers have become a real *issue* in our schools. They've been banned, and un-banned time after time, and the argument about whether these historic items of joy and delight are actually a danger to our precious young, continues to rage!

New headteacher in Somerset lifts conker ban saying 'it's harmless if handled safely'

[*BBC News October 12 2006*]

A ban on playground conker games has been lifted at a Somerset school after the arrival of a new headteacher.

Conker battles were outlawed five years ago at a school near Bridgwater, because of concerns about injuries to the pupils. But newly-appointed headmistress Catherine G said: 'It's a harmless game if handled safely. I think we want children to spend time outside; a lot of children spend their time indoors these days.'

The children have been having lessons in how to prepare conkers for play.

One pupil told the BBC: 'I just think that if we were not playing conkers, it'll just die out in the end.'

Mrs G added: 'I think a lot of fun can be had playing conkers so I decided it was time to change things around and have conkers.'

Conker ban over nut allergy

Conkers have been banned at a school in Scotland because of worries pupils with nut allergies could get ill if they touch them.

Menstrie Primary head Veronica O'Grady made the rule after parents of allergy sufferers said they were worried about nuts being around in the classroom. Ms O'Grady asked a specialist at a hospital if conkers could be a problem for allergic kids and was told yes.

The school has been a peanut-free zone for several years.

Two pupils at the school have a nut allergy which can be life-threatening for them if they come into contact with nuts.

Pupils at Menstrie found in possession of the banned tree nuts will have them confiscated by teachers. But they'll get their conkers back at home time.

Ms O'Grady told CBBC Newsround Online the school has had no complaints so far. 'Having taken medical advice I can't ignore it. If anyone wants to talk about it further they can come and ask me and I'll explain it to them.

'It's rather extreme but if you do something on medical advice you are doing it for the safety of the children,' said Ms O'Grady.

Police stopped and searched three children who had been collecting conkers in Littlehampton, West Sussex, and confiscated a bag containing about 100 horse-chestnuts.

Cuddling the class pet is cruel, RSPCA tells school

Clutching the school guinea pig or charting the growth of tadpoles in a jar has, for generations, been many children's first encounter with the natural world.

But the practice of keeping animals in school is endangered and may even become extinct, if RSPCA guidance is enforced, *The Times* reported in May, 2008.

Allowing small children, and even smaller creatures, to interact during lessons can be cruel, according to the animal welfare charity. It says that the shrieks and grabbing hands of affectionate but boisterous pupils make the classroom a frightening and noisy place for pets.

They could have added that animals should no longer be termed 'pets', according to the most enlightened thinking. They are 'animal companions'.

Don't use the S-word. This is a place of learning, not a school

When is a school not a school? When it is a 'place for learning', we learned from *The Times* at the beginning of 2009.

Watercliffe Meadow Primary in Sheffield has adopted the new phraseology because it thinks that the word school may have negative connotations for pupils and parents.

Linda Kingdon, the headteacher, said that the change would bring the school (or place of learning) close to real life. But critics condemned it as laughable political correctness.

Sorry, Romeo, but you're not allowed to kiss her

A new rule could mean productions of classics like *Romeo and Juliet* being axed because of love scenes vital to the plot, reported *The Sun* in February, 2007.

Education watchdogs said this ludicrous measure was designed to prevent abuse of pupils.

But teachers and MPs blasted it as yet more daft interference by officials.

They said there was no point in staging a romance unless pupils could act the love scenes. And they vowed to act last night after plans to remove 'intimate physical contact' from plays were revealed.

A chaste peck or hug will be as far as the passion goes under new rules from the Qualifications, Curriculum and Assessment Authority in Wales.

And its English counterpart is now looking at imposing the 'positive initiative'.

The Welsh QCA said: 'Drama teachers must think about what gestures and movements are appropriate and cut or adapt plays if they have to. In most cases, a peck on the cheek or an embrace can communicate the required emotion.'

They also call for strong language to be censored. But teachers say kids see far worse on TV soaps. And they fear the plans will strip classics like Shakespeare's masterpieces of their meaning.

Margaret Higgins, of the National Association for Teaching of Drama, said: 'You can't cut scenes like the kiss in *Romeo and Juliet*. It's a crucial moment. If it isn't fit subject matter, perhaps they should put 'East Enders' on after the watershed.'

Shadow education secretary David Willetts said: 'Drama is full of passion and violence and kids grow and learn by acting these plays out.'

Last night Education Secretary Ruth Kelly insisted great drama would remain on the curriculum. She said: 'It is vital children learn the classics. That will not change.'

Energy drinks have too much energy

[Northampton Chronicle and Echo December 12 2008]

Energy drinks could be banned from the playground of a Northamptonshire school following concerns from teachers that pupils were drinking them 'routinely'.

Ross P, headteacher of the sports college concerned, said he is worried about the health implications for pupils who drink products such as Red Bull and Relentless before school starts, meaning they are not being used as an energy supplement for strenuous activity.

Mr P said he and other teachers had discovered drinks cans around the school premises, and he had confiscated a can from a boy who had just got off the bus into school, so had not undergone any physical activity to warrant needing the drink.

He said: 'I think there's a bit of a street culture about it to be honest. They are attractively packaged cans for young people.'

He added: 'All staff will advise if there seems to be a change in a pattern of a pupil's behaviour. I came across a lad drinking one of these drinks fairly early in the day; I don't think it's the best way to start the school day.'

The head said he would be watching the situation closely to see if any of his students suffer any effects of hyperactivity or irritability, and may ban the drinks if he notices anything unusual.

The school first raised the issue in its December newsletter advising against the 'significant and worrying' health concerns of the drinks, and the head said he has received no adverse response from parents, adding: 'I can't control what young people do and it's not for me to make a judgment on that [precisely what he was doing] but I have a responsibility to advise parents that we have concerns about these high-energy drinks.'

The World Health Organisation (WHO) said it has no specific guidelines on energy drinks.

Killer chocolate

A 92-year-old school governor has been banned from handing chocolate to pupils on health and safety grounds – and has had to opt for raisins instead, the *Western Daily Press* has discovered.

Big-hearted Hartley P has given youngsters KitKat bars every week at the school in Falmouth, Cornwall, for more than 10 years. But on the first day of the new term, he was told the chocolate would have to go because it was against the school's healthy eating policy.

Milk, too, can make you fat

[*The Scotsman* March 26 2009]

Children as young as three have been banned from drinking full-fat milk in Scottish nurseries and schools.

A Scottish Government directive, which is being phased in at all primary and secondary schools, prevents pupils from drinking the 'high-calorie' milk, replacing it with the semi-skimmed variety.

Last night, health experts raised concerns that the Scottish Government's healthy-eating drive was excessive and denied young children the essential fats they need as part of their normal development.

Dr Rafe Bundy, a lecturer in nutrition at Glasgow University, said: 'Full-fat milk has 4 per cent fat and it is actually a low-fat food. When you think about it, compared with a lot of foods milk is low-fat because it is mainly water: it is water and vitamins and calcium and protein.'

The Scottish Government's decision is part of a range of healthy-eating measures to improve the diet of children in Scotland, amid fears of an obesity crisis.

Mind that mortar board

Graduating students at Anglia Ruskin university were banned from throwing mortar boards into the air as part of celebrations as they might injure themselves. *The Times* reported this grave risk to health in May 2008.

Health and safety 'no' to self-helpers

Community groups in Edinburgh hit with hefty cleaning bills for using city schools have offered to sweep up after themselves instead – only to be told it was against health and safety rules. Education bosses are to charge groups and children's holiday clubs a total cleaning bill of around £12,000 a year for groups using the capital's 30 school buildings which are open during holidays.

The council says it needs to comply with strict regulations, and will require groups to pay £6.76 an hour for professional cleaners. 'The nature of the chemicals and some of the equipment used means that we must use a professional cleaning company for safety reasons,' a spokesman told the *Edinburgh Evening News* in April 2009.

And we end this chapter on a refreshing voice of reason...

'Cotton wool culture stops children from taking risks'

[*Daily Mail March 4 2009*]

Youngsters are failing to learn to recover from life's knocks because a 'cotton wool' culture prevents them from experiencing hardships, a headteachers' leader has warned.

David Hanson said children are becoming increasingly protected from risk and failure, preventing them from learning how to bounce back from setbacks.

The Head of the Independent Association of Preparatory Schools also criticised the widespread idea that children should be happy and satisfied at all times.

Mr Hanson, whose organisation represents hundreds of private prep schools, said: 'I worry we are becoming risk averse, that we are becoming averse to failure.

'Risk and failure are opposite sides of the coins of success and achievement. If we want achievement then we have to occasionally fall down.'

Nanny State edicts

Bird-lovers have been banned from feeding ducks at a popular village pond in the latest 'nanny state' crackdown, said the *Daily Express* in October, 2007.

The local council claims the practice is spreading disease and attracting vermin. It has put up signs around the pond at Oakley, Hampshire, saying: 'We would be grateful if in future you do not feed the ducks. Bread is not good for them and any uneaten bread encourages rats.'

Villager Hilary B, 75, said: 'Children have fed the ducks for donkey's years and it is part of their heritage. It's true that the more you feed the ducks the more droppings they produce but I've never heard of children getting a disease.'

Mrs B was paid £70 a year by the council to feed the ducks pellets every day until last year. She described the ban as symptomatic of a 'nanny state' culture.

She said: 'The sign says that feeding bread to ducks can be bad for them but I think we have the healthiest ducks in the world.'

Oldham parents Steve and Mandy B got a telling off from a council official after trying to take photographs in a local park – of their own daughter. Baby Rebecca was on the swings when a council employee told them taking photographs was illegal. The council later admitted their employee had misinterpreted the rules. We heard of a similar ruling banning a granny from taking a picture of her grandchild in a swimming pool.

Her gnomes were not indecent after all

According to the *Sunday Times* in April 2009, gnome-collector, Sandra S was told to put clothes on three of her favourite ornaments because they were deemed offensive.

The 64-year-old initially hid their modesty with T-shirts and cowboy hats but later removed the clothing following advice from a local police officer that she needn't have bothered.

The grandmother, from the West Midlands, said, 'I had a telephone call from Bromsgrove District Council who said could I please cover them up because they were offensive to my neighbour. A spokesman for the council later quipped that council guidelines were statutory, not statuary, and did not explicitly grant authority over 'gnome-related' incidents.

Flags were health risk

A street's display of St George's flags were taken down by a local council because they might fly off and obscure the windscreens of passing cars. Bureaucrats sent out a workman in a truck equipped with a cherry-picker to take all the flags down, accompanied by policemen in an unmarked van, saying they were a health and safety risk (the flags, not the policemen).

The flags had been put up by members of the local Orange Lodge in Liverpool, in a main road which is decorated with Irish flags every St Patrick's Day. Liverpool City Council insisted there was a risk the 3ft-long red and white crosses could blow off.

Buxom barmaids exposed too much
[*Mail online August 2005*]
Buxom barmaids across Europe were in danger of being forced to cover up because the EU was worried they were being exposed to too much sun.

The Germans were particularly worried that this ruling would mean an end to the traditional low-cut outfits known as dirndls worn by barmaids at the Munich beer festival. The mayor was outraged. 'A waitress is no longer allowed to wander round a beer garden with a plunging neckline. I would not want to enter a beer garden under these conditions,' he said.

The European Union Optical Radiation Directive was originally designed to protect employees working near X-ray machines or industrial equipment. The European Commission then added sunlight as another potential danger.

Too anxious to save a life
A coastguard who risked his life to save a teenage girl stranded on a cliff ledge resigned after he was criticised for breaching health and safety rules during the rescue. Paul W, 44, was so concerned for the 13-year-old girl that he clambered down to her in a gale-force wind without waiting to fit a safety harness, according to a report in *The Times* in January 2008.

The father of three, who was hailed as a hero and received an award for stopping the girl falling 300 feet as she waited for an RAF rescue helicopter, announced he was leaving the service after 13 years.

Officials at the Maritime and Coastguard Agency said that Mr W had breached health and safety regulations because he had not been roped up for the descent. A spokesman said the rules were in place because the agency did not want any 'dead heroes'.

The coastguard said, 'I am very sad that I have to leave because I loved my job, but it is one of those things. You save a life and this is how they treat you. I am sorry, but I would not leave any 13-year-old girl hanging off a cliff.'

Councillors in Slough ignited a blazing row last year after banning bonfires and burning Guys from their November 5th celebrations. Critics accused the council of being too worried about excluding ethnic minorities, but the council said the move was designed to help reduce their carbon footprint and to look after the environment.

And then there are trees. Sadly trees do fall down sooner or later, so you can't blame councils for worrying about their potential for landing on somebody, or something, when this happens. Still...

Pear drops

A pair of pear trees in a park in Worcester have been cordoned off to prevent their fruit falling on the heads of passers-by, reported the *Daily Telegraph* recently. The trees, which stand 30-feet high, have not caused a single problem in 50 years, but have been enclosed within tape and a barrier. Signs were pinned to each tree which said: 'Warning, pears falling!'

Ancient oak to get the axe

A 200-year-old oak tree is for the chop because a council fears it could be sued if it falls on anyone.

The mighty Luccombe Oak is believed to have stood in Crewkerne, Somerset, for around 200 years but it has been blighted by a fungus on its roots.

Despite a campaign by residents to keep the tree Crewkerne Town Council decided that it must be felled. The council said it was following a warning from its insurer that the council would be liable should the tree fall and injure someone.

And finally another of those dreaded conker stories. Only this time potentially killer cherries are involved too, in this story from the *Daily Mail*, October 2006:

Rather than risk children damaging themselves or property by collecting conkers, Newcastle upon Tyne City Council is responding to residents' requests to get to them first.

Taxpayers are funding the operation by the council's environmental services team to use a cherry picker crane to strip trees bare of conkers before children can get their hands on them. Officials insist it is a sensible safety request and they are only reacting to public demand. But members of the public have been stunned by the sight of the conker-picking team at work.

The council has refused to reveal the cost of the operation which last year led to more than 10 horse chestnut trees being 'picked' before the children could get to them. The conkers are then passed to local schools to be used for organized conker fighting.

The environmental services delivery manager responsible for maintaining trees in public spaces, said: 'We look after all the trees and picking conkers and things like cherries and pears is part of the service.

'At the moment we are getting a lot of complaints from residents in the city because of the cherries on the trees. They cause a lot of mess and they're very slippy. This means we go out and pick the cherries before they fall.'

The Great – and risky – Outdoors

At home, you're on your own, as it were. But as soon as we step outside into a public space, it's a completely different matter. Suddenly our personal health and safety becomes the concern of myriad officials all desperate to protect us from our own recklessness. And the great outdoors is positively brimming with natural and man-made threats like, er, trees, see-saws and ducks.

Children's play-grounds are, understandably, a great cause of consternation to the authorities. Play equipment, in particular, seems to attract trouble. We particularly liked the following story in which a council, literally, moved the goal posts...

Council move children's goal posts over 'health and safety fears'

[*Daily Mail, February 22 2007*]

What's white, wide and waist-high, but still potentially invisible? The answer, according to a county council, is a set of goalposts used by children playing football.

They ordered their removal from the small field where they were standing – in case walkers fell over them. Astonished local people were told that ramblers using a public footpath across the field might have their heads bent over a map and not see the obstacle.

Then, of course, there was the danger to people out at night.

But the decision by Cheshire County Council has been branded an own goal by families whose children use the field, part of a play area in Alderley Edge. Philip R, a father of three, said: 'Councils are constantly bleating about the obesity problem our children are facing and then they go and mess about with facilities aimed at combating it.

'It is preposterous to remove goalposts because someone could bump into them at night. By that rule, every obstacle from public bins to lamp posts is an impediment that could cause harm if someone didn't look where they were going at night.'

He added: 'What you have to ask is: "Why would people want go out walking across fields in the middle of the night?".'

Mary Maczkowiak, chairman of Alderley Edge Parish Council called the officials 'killjoys' and said most right-minded people would walk around the outside of the small field because it was too muddy in the centre.

She said: 'I noticed the goalposts had disappeared and after further investigation found out that they had been removed after a visit from the local rights of way officer. They must have just come round and done a sweep. It is so ridiculous – there are far more important issues with footpaths around here.'

The fate of the goalposts was sealed after an inspection by county council officials. They ordered Macclesfield Borough Council, which owns the field, to move them.

One consolation for local people is that the council is planning to improve the play area and will be consulting them before deciding what to put there.

In the meantime, walkers can stride fearlessly across the site – so long as they can see their way past all the other hazards – the basketball net, swings, slide and seesaw – that are still there.

Village seesaw can damage your eyesight

A seesaw in the play area of the Cotswold village of Bledington was ordered to be removed after bringing enjoyment to local children for more than 40 years. In all that time, there hadn't been a single accident, but that didn't affect the judgement of a Playing Fields Association officer who deemed it a danger. The swings had to go too... because they faced the sun and therefore posed a risk to the health of children's eyes.

Mayor's flag can be dangerous

[*The Sun June 28 2008*]

The town flag on an official Mayor's limo has been banned in case it hurts someone. The eight-inch coat of arms, referred to as a flag, but actually a crest that sits on the front of the roof – was branded a health and safety risk by a borough official.

Councillors were warned by their 'democratic services manager' that it might fall off if the car is driven above a certain speed. 'We must avoid any chance of damaging other cars and inconveniencing other road users.'

The ruling by Maidstone Borough Council in Kent came after it took delivery of a new £40,000 chauffeur-driven Lexus. The decision not to fit the crest – eight inches high and five wide – stunned the Mayor. The mum of three, a Lib-Dem councillor, warned: 'There is a certain protocol when the mayor arrives at an event. If the car is not instantly recognised it may be directed into the wrong place.'

But a council insider scoffed yesterday: 'The flag has never fallen off before or caused any accidents, so I don't know why it is being brought up now. It's health and safety gone mad.' A taxpayer added: 'How can a little flag on the mayor's car be a risk? There are enough potholes around here to worry about.'

No, nobody's actually had an accident, but you never know

A slide in a playground in Birmingham has been condemned as a safety hazard, even though no one has been injured on it in 50 years of use, and no parent has ever complained about it.

Birmingham Botanical Gardens decided to replace the 10ft-high steel slide after a health and safety audit raised concerns about its height. [reported in *The Week* June 14 2008]

It seems there is nothing, no matter how innocuous, that does not have the potential to stir up trouble. Take the following...

Mr and Mrs B, from Warwickshire, put a tiny, tinkling wind chime up in their garden to help distract them from the noise of aircraft flying overhead on their approach to Coventry airport, a mile away. So imagine their surprise when they were ordered to move the one-inch diameter chime by Rugby Council after an investigation costing more than £1,000.

A group of 30 children, all aged under three, raised nearly £150 for charity by toddling through their local park. Their achievement was somewhat marred when they subsequently received a bill for £36 from their local council in Dorset, for the cost of checking whether the event needed policing.

Earmuffs for pig feeders

According to *The Week* for May 30, 2009, farmers have been advised to wear earmuffs when feeding pigs, to protect themselves from 'dangerously' loud squeals. The Health and Safety Executive says the noise of hungry pigs could be as damaging to hearing as that of a chainsaw or power drill, and suggests using mechanical feeders to avoid exposure altogether.

Strawberries squashed by health & safety rules
[*Daily Mail June 4 2009*]

For most visitors the only injury likely to befall them is a pricked finger or a little sunburn. But that hasn't stopped health and safety bosses claiming pick-your-own fruit farms could be hiding a host of hazards within their hedgerows.

One of the country's most popular strawberry farms has announced it is to close to the public after being ordered to 'radically refurbish' its land following a risk assessment.

The firm, in Cornwall, has been told it needs to install

walkways and bridges between a row of strawberries, cordon potholes in the fields and install handrails near open ditches.

This popular attraction opened in 1945 and was one of the first pick-your-own fruit farms in Britain. It will continue to grow strawberries and make its own range of jams and conserves.

A spokesman for the farm said: 'To us it's a pick-your-own farm but to the insurers and the health and safety people it's a strawberry factory. The insurers want us to cotton wool the place.'

Beware plastic flowers
[*Daily Mail August 8 2008*]
Grieving families in Keynsham, near Bristol, have been told not to put plastic flowers in a garden of remembrance because they pose a health and safety risk. Workmen removed several displays from a cemetery in the town and moved them to the chapel of rest for collection by loved ones.

In response to uproar, a council official said, 'We have always had a ban on plastic flowers in the garden but had not enforced it fully until staff complained that cutting the grass was becoming difficult. It became more of a problem over time, with more people leaving more and more mementoes. We also have to consider health and safety. If the flowers get caught up in the lawnmower the bits of plastic flying around could be very dangerous.'

In June Croydon Council banned plastic flowers from an elderly persons' accommodation block because they, too, were deemed a risk.

Horses must wear nappies

Horses which pull the popular landau carriages up and down Blackpool seafront must now wear nappies to keep the streets clean, the *Daily Telegraph* reported in September 2008.

Council chiefs imposed the condition on owners of the town's famous horse-drawn carriages after complaints about the high level of smelly and unsightly droppings the horses left behind. They made it a condition of the operators' licences that all horses should be fitted with the nappies, or dung catchers, which were designed by the RSPCA.

But some operators are failing to comply with the new regulation and have been warned they will lose their licences unless they clean up their act. The deputy leader of Blackpool Council said that a recent visit to the promenade showed many of the horses' backsides were still exposed.

One slip, no injury and it's the last post for Ardmore

[*Times online July 10 2006*]

The nearest supermarket involves a 200-mile round trip and visiting the bank means 50 miles each way, but until now the mail has always got through.

For more than 100 years, postmen have walked without incident along a one-and-a-half mile track by the edge of a sea loch to deliver letters and parcels to the small Highland township of Ardmore.

But two days after a relief postman slipped, the Royal Mail withdrew its service on 'health and safety' grounds. It claims the footpath is 'fundamentally dangerous' and could put the lives of postmen at risk, although a mother who lives in Ardmore walks the route on most days with her six-year-old daughter and her three-year-old son.

Residents on the rocky peninsula, where the former paratrooper John Ridgway set up an adventure school almost 40 years ago, claim that the postman did not see a doctor, and continued his round after the incident.

A report for Postcomm, the independent regulator, concluded that the track was hazardous, and an offer from the local authority to upgrade the path was rejected.

But the council continues to encourage holidaymakers to use the route and an independent report concluded it was well maintained and 'an easy walk'.

George M, one of the four postmen who have worked on the route regularly over the past 40 years, said of the footpath: 'It's punishing and it's tiring, but I enjoyed it.'

Mr R, 68, who retired in 2003 said: 'Because one person said he slipped, it has allowed Royal Mail to escape from its obligation. What is being done is purely for financial reasons, and if the Royal Mail gets away with it, where next?

'As far as I know the relief postman did not see a doctor and continued his walk.'

A Royal Mail spokesman said: 'The only factor that motivated Royal Mail's actions is concern for the health and safety of our people.' She understood that the postman suffered concussion and that the route was unacceptable because at some points there was no mobile phone reception.

Last year, Royal Mail suspended about 700 services on health and safety grounds.

Washing line fear

Sheerness Holiday Park in Kent have banned campers from putting up washing lines to dry their clothes because they endanger life and limb. A report in the *Daily Telegraph* on May 7 2009 said campers were up in arms, demanding their washing lines back and saying the rules were ridiculous. There has never been a washing line accident at the camp.

Council tells helpful pensioner: keep off our grass

[*The Times October 17 2008*]
A pensioner has been ordered to stop trimming the grass verge outside his house – because he is making it too tidy.

Brian H, 72, has been mowing, weeding and edging the verge for eight years. But now officials at Herefordshire Council, which owns the land, have written to him saying that he must return it to its original state within 28 days or they will send workmen to undo his efforts and charge him.

Mr H said: 'Somebody from the council said if it was too tidy people might not feel they could walk over it. It's absolutely ridiculous'.

Don't lock the shed, thieves won't like it

[*Daily Mail and most national papers*]

Allotment holders are being urged not to lock their sheds – in case burglars damage them while breaking in.

They have been warned that padlocks force robbers to smash their way through doors and windows damaging the council-owned buildings in the process.

The advice means allotment holders would have to leave their expensive equipment unsecured overnight, despite a spate of recent break-ins.

The West Country local authority claims its initiative will save taxpayers' money because fewer sheds will have to be repaired or replaced.

Twig that was 5mm too thick

A pensioner was told to book a special rubbish truck to dispose of a small branch from his garden because it was 5mm too thick.

Jack H, 70, put the 'tiddly' branch in his bin after cutting down a small tree in his garden. But bin men refused to empty it.

When he contacted his local council at Leeds, he was told that the branch, measuring 3.5 cm in diameter, was 5mm too thick to be allowed in his brown bin for garden waste.

The council suggested he book a collection truck or take the branch to his local dump. He decided to keep it for posterity.

Hanging basket threatened mayhem

A tenant faces a ban on putting up hanging baskets outside her flat – because of health and safety fears, the *Bucks Free Press* revealed.

Housing chiefs told stunned Sharon K the six baskets on her ground-floor flat posed a 'potential risk' to safety. And the 43-year-old could also be told to move plant pots from the communal area at the block of flats in Beaconsfield.

Asthma sufferer Sharon told the *Bucks Free Press* the move was 'over the top' – and said it left her in tears as her plants were her 'little enjoyment. I think it's stupid. They're not a risk – they have been there since I moved in 2000'.

Window box ban angers residents

A notice ordering the removal of window boxes at an east London housing complex because of safety fears has caused anger among people living there.

The management committee, made up of residents at Bow Quarter, has told occupants the pots will be removed if they do not comply. The committee said the decision was made after being told the pots may cause problems with insurance. But residents say forcibly removing the pots would amount to theft.

Beware palm trees ahead!

Palm trees at Torbay, once an emblem of the English Riviera, are now emblematic of the modern obsession with health and safety, the press reported in June 2006.

The palms had long appeared in posters promoting Torbay's mild climate, but a council official wrote to the local chamber of trade saying the trees were a potential hazard because their sharp leaves could injure eyes or faces. Faced with the inevitable storm of anger, a councillor said, 'It's a bit like keeping tigers, they are beautiful to look at, but you wouldn't want them wandering the streets.' One commentator asked, 'Where does it stop? Will we be banning rose bushes from public gardens in case people hurt themselves?'

The council's last word was that they didn't want to ban palm trees outright, just site them as prominently as they could, but in an appropriate area. 'It's something we have got to be careful about,' he added.

Food isn't always good for you

None of us can do without food, and as well as being a physiological imperative, it can also be one of life's true pleasures. And, like conkers, food has many connotations that are nostalgic. We always associate certain tastes with certain people and occasions... certain *home-made* tastes that is. I don't ever recall hearing anyone wax lyrical about tins of beans, packet soups or pop-tarts, yet the smell of a baking cake sends most of us straight back to our grandmothers' kitchens and the scent of apples bubbling in a pan and a combination of certain spices will remind us of a certain time of year, and the person who was standing beside us.

Of course care must be taken with food. Some people do have potentially life-threatening allergies, and nobody wants to put something in their mouths that's been prepared in an unhygienic fashion. Still, the current trend for banning people from taking home-made dishes as gifts for elderly people in care homes and hospitals seems particularly cruel: a cake or lasagne that's been made with love is highly unlikely to have been made with germs. And don't get us started on all those regulations affecting cake sales...

Polystyrene eggs are better for you

At Easter 2009, pupils at a school near Aberdeen were banned from taking eggs to school because of potential allergies. They had traditionally painted hard-boiled eggs as part of an annual competition. But the school is now facing criticism after replacing them with polystyrene versions because parents of two pupils revealed their children were allergic to eggs.

Letters were sent to parents which showed a cheerful dancing egg next to a stern warning not to take actual eggs into school.

Beware! This box of eggs contains... egg

[*Mail on Sunday January 25 2009*]

In these health-conscious times food companies are increasingly keen to warn consumers if ingredients may cause allergic reactions. But one firm has gone a step further by advising shoppers that its boxes of eggs contain... egg.

The Happy Egg Company's six-pack of eggs – which features the company's name and is decorated with a picture of an egg and a cartoon chicken – contains the message 'allergy advice: contains egg' inside the lid of the boxes.

Even worse! This milk bottle contains, er, milk

Another national newspaper reports similar stories:

In a nation overwhelmed by health and safety paranoia, shops go to great lengths to protect themselves from litigious customers. So we've had bags of peanuts warning they contain nuts and egg boxes telling the unwary that inside are… eggs.

Asda, it emerged yesterday, really is milking this trend for all its worth. On the side of its plastic milk bottles, under the heading 'Allergy advice' is the warning: 'Contains milk'. Bars of milk chocolate, too, now carry warnings by the makers of this unsuspected and potentially dangerous ingredient in their product.

Cheese and onion sandwiches must be frozen

The traditional Beacon Hotel public house in the Midlands has stopped selling cheese and onion cobs after 80 years after health and safety inspectors pointed out that they should be refrigerated. The cobs had, in recent years, been wrapped in cling-film. Landlord John Hughes was reported as saying: 'We keep the pub like a museum.' He said tourists appreciated the pub's original features and the cheese and onion cobs 'are a little part of that heritage.'

Bones are not food

A butcher in West Yorkshire was told he could lose his licence if he sold bones to dog owners. Bones are classed as a waste by-product, not food, and as such must not be sold, but incinerated instead.

Children's pancake race axed by health and safety killjoys

[*Thisislondon.uk February 5 2008*]

A cathedral city's traditional pancake race has been scrapped because of fears over health and safety.

The event was revived 11 years ago and since then crowds have gathered in the centre of Ripon, North Yorkshire, on Shrove Tuesday to watch school children running down a cobbled street flipping pancakes as they go.

The start is signalled by the ringing of the cathedral's ancient 'pancake bell' at 11 am on the day. The bell, originally sounded to call worshippers to make their confession before the start of Lent, has been rung at that time for at least 600 years.

However, organisers have reluctantly scrapped the popular pancake race this year because of mounting costs and bureaucracy linked to health and safety rules.

Charity cakes must be insured, says council

A woman who raised hundreds of pounds for charity by selling tea and cakes in her front garden was so successful that her local council is to treat her as a 'business' and has ordered her to take out a £5 million insurance policy.

Diane T set out tables and chairs in the garden of her two-bedroom holiday home at a chalet park near Cleethorpes, Lincolnshire, to sell her lemon drizzle and walnut cakes to passers by.

Her 30p buns and £1.20 tea-and-scone offering helped raise around £900 for the Royal National Lifeboat Institution.

Councillors told not to eat during Ramadan meetings

Councillors have been asked not to eat or drink in committee meetings while Muslims fast during Ramadan, according to a report in the *Daily Telegraph*.

Members of Tower Hamlets Council in east London, where 36 per cent of the population is Muslim, were sent an email asking them to abide by the restrictions.

Fruit and nuts....

[*Western Daily Press June 27 2008*]
A wholesaler has been banned from selling a batch of kiwi fruits by EU regulations because they are … one millimetre too small.

Market trader Tim D was told his perfectly-healthy fruits failed to meet strict European standards for size and weight.

Inspectors found some of his stock weighed just four grams less than the minimum EU requirement – and slapped him with a written warning prohibiting their sale.

Pudsey Bear threat to children's health

[*Bristol Evening Post November 13 2008*]
A Bristol headteacher has banned hundreds of kids from baking cakes for Children in Need on health and safety grounds.

Pupils were due to bake Pudsey Bear-themed cakes at home and sell them to their classmates today to raise money for the charity as they have for the last 28 years.

But the headteacher stepped in and banned the event at the last minute citing health and safety reasons. She claimed the homemade buns would not meet strict hygiene standards and risked sparking allergic reactions among pupils.

The 1,500 pupils at the school in Mangotsfield have now been told not to bring in their own cakes for the national charity event.

Parents and students aged 11-18 years have branded the ban 'utterly stupid'.

Car dealer Andy H, 32, who sends his 14-year-old stepson to the school said: 'It's completely ridiculous that they have done this as baking cakes is perfectly safe. I have some really happy memories of the times we have baked cakes in the last few years.

'They are killjoys who have spoiled so many children's fun and I just can't get my head round it.'

A sixth-form film studies pupil added: 'We're taught to bake cakes in classes at school from the age of 13. It's so bizarre that they should teach us how to bake them and then suddenly ban us from doing it to raise money.

'All the pupils are well capable of making them hygienically and leaving out any potentially allergic ingredients. My parents feel exactly the same way that it's utterly stupid taking health and safety this far to stop us from having fun.'

Pupils at the school have baked cakes alongside other fundraising activities such as dressing up since the BBC appeal started in 1980. But the headteacher broke 28 years of tradition and introduced the ban on Tuesday this week by warning pupils not to bring in cakes.

It was feared that ingredients like nuts and artificial additives, such as gluten, could make pupils ill. Instead, school cooks will bake hundreds of fairy cakes and gingerbread men in the canteen which will then be sold to pupils.

Another parent said: 'This is PC gone mad and it just becomes worse and worse. We have always done this for fundraising events during the year as long as I can remember. Now all of a sudden we cannot even do this and let our kids bake cakes and they have to eat those dull things made in the canteen.'

Headteacher Tamryn S defended the decision and claimed there would be other ways for the pupils to raise money. She said: 'I have a very important job to do and that's ensuring the health and safety of all my pupils.

'I suddenly thought about this and realised that my kids have a range of allergies and asked myself, "what if one of them eats something they shouldn't?" I think we handled the situation really well and the parents we've spoken to have been really supportive.

'I feel very strongly I have made the right decision.'

Hospital bans staff from making their own tea

[*Daily Telegraph July 18 2008*]
Hospital staff have been banned from making 'unofficial' cups of tea and coffee to cut costs and save the environment.

Sandwich scuppers round-the-world skipper and cakes must be destroyed

[*Daily Telegraph August 29 2008*]

The skipper of a record-breaking powerboat was given a warning after being spotted eating a sandwich on his boat.

Pete B described the health and safety culture as 'out of control' after being threatened with a possible £50,000 fine. Passengers gave him the snack while on a pleasure trip. But Health and Safety officials viewed the sandwich as 'payment in kind'.

Meanwhile, cakes are destroyed instead of being eaten in the name of health and safety, according to the *Scottish Daily Record*.

The Scottish Women's Rural Institute have banned the consumption of cakes and scones entered in competitions, insisting that all baked goods are destroyed immediately following judging.

Ice cream toppings banned amid health and safety fears

In January 2008, the *Daily Express* reported: A luxury ice cream chain is refusing to pour chocolate sauce and other toppings over its cones because of health and safety fears.

In another example of nanny state rules blighting Britain, world-famous Morellis Gelato claims its popular toppings pose a serious hazard to the public if they fall on the floor.

The Italian chain, with parlours at Harrods and Selfridges in London and on the seafront in the well-to-do resort of

Broadstairs, Kent, has banned staff adding little extras because customers might slip over.

Instead they are given the ice cream with the topping – such as chocolate and strawberry sauce, chopped nuts and pieces of fresh fruit – served in a separate tub.

More food risks

In May, 2009, the *Daily Telegraph* report the case of a grandfather banned from buying fish and chips for friends in a sheltered housing block after wardens ruled that the food might pose a health and safety risk after it got cold.

George P, 72, was ordered to stop his weekly lunch run for fellow residents at the complex though the drive back from the fish and chip shop takes only five minutes.

Managers at the council-run centre in Norwich decided to suspend the Wednesday lunch club after attending a food hygiene course. They said the lunch would not resume until they could secure heat-proof boxes to protect the fish and chips during the short run from the shop to plate.

Meanwhile, we read of the elderly recipients of meals-on-wheels in Gloucestershire who are no longer allowed paper napkins lest they mistake them for food and choke on them.

Chop softly, please

Finally, a butcher was told in January 2009 by Barking Council that he chops up his meat too loudly. He's been told to soundproof his shop.

Not so smashing

The tradition of smashing plates in Greek restaurants is dying out because owners are frightened of being sued by customers hit by shards of flying crockery – to the disappointment of those who regard the plate-smashing an integral part of the experience.

A *Daily Telegraph* report revealed that some restaurateurs have replaced plates with less dramatic alternatives. 'We're throwing flowers now,' said the owner of one restaurant in north London. 'It's not as messy and if you hit someone, it doesn't really matter. We used to smash plates for many, many years, since we opened about 25 years ago, but we stopped because we were worried about being sued.'

Over the centuries, breaking plates has become linked with the Greek concept of *kefi* (high spirits and fun). Some say that it wards off evil spirits. Others maintain that plates broken during a wedding reception symbolise good luck and a happy, lasting marriage.

Many owners complained that customers' escalating rowdiness had added to their anxieties. Fights have been known to start after fragments of crockery landed in other customers' moussaka.

Safety inspectors, not surprisingly, said that the restaurateurs were right to be cautious. The food policy officer at the Chartered Institute of Environmental Health – the professional body for local authority inspectors – said: 'It's one of those things that seem great fun, but there are hidden dangers in it.

'Plate shards can do quite a lot of damage, especially to the eye. You also have the potential for shards of crockery to go into food. The people running the restaurant should do a risk assessment.'

Chip shop smells of ... fish and chips

In November 2007 Sky News reported that a chip shop owner was investigated because his shop smelled of fish and chips. A council spokesman explained they were obliged to look into the complaint about the shop in Wakefield, West Yorkshire.

She said the owner had been asked to check that the odour extraction system was working properly. It was certainly not a case that a fish and chip shop should not be allowed to smell of fish and chips.

Mind your language!

Researching this chapter has probably come up with the craziest (no, can't say that), er... stupidest (no, no, no, definitely offensive) um.... most bizarre examples of people worrying about other people's feelings being hurt by the inappropriate use of language. We honestly don't wish to upset anybody, but we can't help feeling that in some cases, things have gone a little TOO far. Words can be hurtful, but you'd have to be a person with extremely thin skin to be bruised by some of the following examples. And please try not to giggle too much at the first story in which an innocent attempt to protest about a planning application came up against an insurmountable, virtual barrier...

No erections, please

A Rochdale resident, unhappy with his neighbour's plans to build an extension, was left fuming after two emails of objection were blocked because they contained the word 'erection'. By the time Ray M wrote an email deemed acceptable by the council's software, planning permission for the extension had already been granted. The council later apologised.

... and don't say what you really mean

Councillors in the Lancashire borough of Pendle reacted with fury when officials advised them to stop using the word 'senior' in job advertisements in case people thought they were discriminating against young people.

The Home Office came in for criticism in 2006 after a leaked memo showed that prison officers in charge of young offenders in Wolverhampton were no longer allowed to call them 'prisoners'. Instead, they were to be addressed by their names or called 'young man'. Officers were also banned from talking about 'feeding' offenders. Only the term 'serving meals' was to be used.

But spare a thought for the optician who wasn't allowed to advertise for a diligent employee, because that would deter people who didn't like to pull their weight...

When optician Pauline M wanted to hire a receptionist, she included the words 'hard-working' in the job advert. Sadly, her local Job Centre said the phrase was discriminatory. Mrs M said: 'It seems you daren't ask for a good day's work in this day and age.' This reminds us of Peter Seller's screen depiction of a trade union leader demanding 'A fair week's wage for a fair day's work.'

Don't you call me luvver...

In August 2003, the leader of Bristol City Council issued an edict telling all reception and security staff that they should not address visitors to the Council House as 'love', 'dear' or 'mate'. Instead, everybody must be addressed with deference as 'Sir' or 'Madam'.

Yet for generations Bristolians have addressed each other as 'my luvver' and 'my luv' as a friendly term of greeting. There was a similar story about the supposed sensitivities of visitors to local offices in Newcastle.

You'll enjoy this one...

Quite properly changing the title of Agatha Christie's *Ten Little Niggers* is one thing, but what about this? Enid Blyton's biographer – Barbara Stoney – backed by the Enid Blyton Society has accused publishers of bowing to political correctness. Some characters in Enid Blyton's books have been changed – for example Dame Slap becomes Dame Snap and Fanny and Dick become Frannie and Rick. Commenting on the changes, Barbara Stoney said: 'I just wonder where it will all stop. Do we start updating Jane Austen next, or Dickens?'

Government gets in the POPO

Thousands of pounds are being wasted renaming the controversial Prolific and Other Priority Offender scheme in case the acronym POPO offends Turkish people, says the *Daily Mail*.

'Popo' is an affectionate term used in Turkey to describe a baby's bottom. The scheme has been renamed PPO even though the Turkish embassy expressed surprise that anyone should think that the term would be thought offensive.

And don't even think about discriminating between the genders...

Girls only banned
The 'Girl wanted to share flat' advertisements which used to fill the accommodation to let columns are outlawed by Brussels. Instead, if a group of females want a new housemate, they have to advertise for a 'person', even if the last thing they want is a male slob and under no circumstances would accept a man.

The EU 'gender equality' proposals were supposed to ensure 'sexual equality in access to goods and services' by preventing differentiation between the sexes. Under the same proposals, women drivers would have to pay hundreds of pounds a year more for their car and life insurance. Currently, female drivers are charged up to 30 per cent less than male drivers because they have fewer accidents.

But the European Commission wants to ban the use of gender in assessing premiums and benefits for insurance, pensions and annuities.

Luisella Pavan-Woolfe, the Commission official masterminding the gender equality drive, argued that it would be unacceptable to charge black people more for car insurance even if it could be proved they had more accidents, so it should be equally unacceptable to differentiate between the sexes.

The logical outcome of this policy is that, for the sake of equality of opportunity, good drivers – including the most careful – end up paying more and subsidising the less careful. But why stop at insurance? Maybe lenders should be banned from discriminating against bad risks by charging them higher interest rates – or not granting them a loan at all?

Council staff banned from saying 'man in the street'... in case women are offended
[*Daily Mail August 26 2008*]
The phrase 'man in the street' has been outlawed by a council because it is 'inherently sexist, not a fair reflection of reality, and makes the views or work of women invisible'.

Members and staff of Chichester District Council in West Sussex are instead told to use 'a positive alternative' such as 'the general public'. They are also advised to avoid phrases such as 'manning the switchboard', and the words Mrs, Miss, girl and lady.

Gingerbread persons replace men
[*Wolverhampton Express & Star   October 20 2006*]
A bakery in Kidderminster has been advertising 'ginger persons' and staff have been correcting those asking for a gingerbread man by saying they no longer sell them and can only offer a ginger person.

However, the store manager said, 'It's just a step too far. We have schoolchildren coming in who have asked for a gingerbread man for years. Now I have to tell them they can't have a gingerbread man and they can only have a ginger person. It is just silly really as the gingerbread man has been around for years. You can't discriminate against a biscuit'.

It seems that common sense will prevail in this case, though, with this statement from Greggs who own the bakery, 'A regional manager took the decision to introduce ginger person in some stores in the West Midlands area.

'We don't know why this has happened but we will be speaking to the manager to make sure the name is reverted to gingerbread man. The gingerbread man has been around for 200 years and we have always called it by that name.'

Shamefully, words associated with Christianity, the monarchy and British history have been dropped from a leading children's dictionary. [*Telegraph Online December 8 2008*] Oxford University Press has removed words like 'aisle', 'bishop', 'chapel', 'empire' and 'monarch' from its Junior Dictionary and replaced them with words like 'blog', 'broadband' and 'celebrity'. Dozens of words related to the countryside have also been culled.

The publisher claims the changes have been made to reflect the fact that Britain is a modern, multicultural, multi-faith society. But academics and headteachers said that the changes to the 10,000-word Junior Dictionary could mean that children lose touch with Britain's heritage.

'We have a certain Christian narrative which has given meaning to us over the last 2,000 years. To say it is all relative and replaceable is questionable,' said Professor Alan Smithers, the director of the Centre for Education and Employment at Buckingham University.

'The word selections are a very interesting reflection of the way childhood is going, moving away from our spiritual background and the natural world and towards the world that information technology creates for us.'

End 'ploddledygook' and return to English, say police

[*Daily Telegraph April 17 2009*]

Police are seeking permission to speak in plain English after years of being mocked for jargon, including 'in the affirmative' for 'yes' which has been called 'ploddledygook'.

Constables in Dumfries and Galloway submitted proposals to the Scottish Police Federation conference next week to end 'confusing and irritating' phrases.

The report reads: 'A return to plain English would avoid confusion and doubt about exactly what we say and mean and would benefit the communities we serve.'

You'd perhaps think there was nothing more innocent than a children's nursery rhyme. You'd be very wrong...

Why black sheep are barred and Humpty can't be cracked

Traditional nursery rhymes are being rewritten at nursery schools to avoid causing offence to children, reported *The Times* in March 2006.

Instead of singing 'Baa baa, black sheep' as generations of children have learnt to do, toddlers in Oxfordshire are being taught to sing 'Baa baa, rainbow sheep'.

The move, which critics will seize on as an example of political correctness, was made after the nurseries decided to re-evaluate their approach to equal opportunities.

Stuart Chamberlain, manager of the Family Centre in Abingdon and the Sure Start centre in Sutton Courtenay, Oxfordshire, told the local *Courier Journal* newspaper: 'We have taken the equal opportunities approach to everything we do. This is fairly standard across nurseries. We are following stringent equal opportunities rules. No one should feel pointed out because of their race, gender or anything else.'

In keeping with the new approach, teachers at the nurseries have reportedly also changed the ending of *Humpty Dumpty* so as not to upset the children and dropped the seven dwarfs from the title of *Snow White*.

A spokesman for Ofsted, the watchdog which inspects Sure Start centres, confirmed that centres are expected to 'have regard to anti-discrimination good practice' and that staff should 'actively promote equality of opportunity'.

Gervase Duffield, a Conservative district councillor representing Sutton Courtenay and Appleford, denounced the ban as ridiculous.

'It's the sort of thing that people continually do nowadays – it's become something of a curse,' he said. 'Why do people waste time and money doing this sort of thing when there are far more important things to think about when it comes to educating our children.'

A mother whose daughter attends the Sure Start nursery at the Family Centre in Abingdon, who did not want to be named, said parents had been astonished by the change.

'"Baa baa, black sheep" has been one of the most well-known nursery rhymes for generations. For people to come along and fiddle with it is ridiculous. What on earth is a rainbow sheep anyway? I've spoken to other parents about it and none of us has ever heard of anyone getting offended by the words "black sheep".' [It's a moot point whether it's insulting to the black community to suggest they would be offended by such a trifling matter]

This is not the first time, however, that the nursery rhyme – written in 1744 satirising the taxes imposed on wool exports – has fallen foul of political correctness. In 2000 Birmingham City Council tried to ban the rhyme, after claiming that it was racist and portrayed negative stereotypes. The council rescinded the ban after black parents said it was ludicrous.

Last year, a nursery school in Aberdeen caused uproar, when teachers changed the lyrics to 'Baa baa, happy sheep'.

Margaret Morrissey, of the National Confederation of Parent Teachers Association, said: 'It's really sad. Children for generations have loved and enjoyed nursery rhymes and it's very sad if adult political correctness doesn't allow them to grow up in an unbiased world.'

A DfES spokesperson said: 'We don't support this approach to the teaching of traditional nursery rhymes, but any such decision would be taken locally.'

And in the same vein...

Reported on BBC News January 29 2009:

'Drunken sailors' have been removed from the lyrics of a nursery rhyme in a government-funded books project. But the Bookstart charity says the re-writing of 'What Shall We Do With the Drunken Sailor?' has 'absolutely nothing to do with political correctness'.

The charity says that the shift from drunken sailor to 'grumpy pirate' was to make the rhyme fit a pirate theme, rather than censorship. 'Put him in the brig until he's sober,' has also been lost in the new version.

Bookstart, a project that encourages parents to read with their young children, has produced a different version – with no references to alcohol-swigging sailors.

Instead the hard-drinking sea shanty has been turned into something gentler, with lyrics such as 'Tickle him till he starts to giggle, Early in the morning.'

The charity has dismissed accusations that this is a politically-correct attempt to avoid the alcohol references, saying that it was a case of re-cycling a familiar tune for reading events that were based on a pirate theme.

'We wanted to find a rhyme which would fit in with this subject and this one has a tune which is instantly recognisable by all,' said a statement from Bookstart.

'The inclusion of action lyrics like "wiggle" and "tickle" offer parents and small children an opportunity to interact, have fun and enjoy acting out the rhyme together.'

In fact, the Drunken Sailor version familiar to children already leaves out some of the saltier verses.

The original includes such suggestions as: 'Shave his belly with a rusty razor', 'Stick him in a bag and beat him senseless' and 'Put him in the hold with the captain's daughter.' The captain's daughter was a euphemism for a lashing from a cat o' nine tails.

This is the latest in a series of disputes over nursery rhymes. Last year, a story based on the 'Three Little Pigs' fairy tale was turned down by a government agency's awards panel as the subject matter could offend Muslims.

A digital book, re-telling the classic story, was rejected by judges who warned that 'the use of pigs raises cultural issues'.

A study in 2004 showed that nursery rhymes exposed children to far more violent incidents than an average evening watching television – including Humpty Dumpty's serious head injury.

Don't be offensive!

A new language guide warns of 'offensive' words and phrases – like 'master copy' and 'patient' because they cause offence. The British Sociological Association says 'master copy' should be replaced with 'top copy' and 'masterful' should be replaced by 'very skilful'.

In January 2009, the *Daily Mail* reported on a survey by thebabywebsite.com that said one in ten parents questioned thought *Snow White and the Seven Dwarfs* should be re-named as the word 'dwarf' is not pc. *Rapunzel* was considered too 'dark' and *Cinderella* too out of date because she was forced to do the housework.

At the same time, *The Sun* reported that a council in Scotland wants librarians re-named 'audience development officers'.

Universities ban 'sexist' Old Masters
[*Daily Telegraph September 20 2008*]
Students and academics are being banned from using the term 'Old Masters' and 'seminal' because of claims they are sexist.

Publishers and universities are outlawing dozens of seemingly innocuous words in case they cause offence. Banned phrases on the list, which was originally drawn up by sociologists, include Old Masters, which has been used for centuries to refer to great painters – almost all of whom were male. It is claimed that the term discriminates against women and should be replaced by 'classic artists'.

This name change is 'politically correct madness'
[*Western Daily Press January 31 2009*]
Since 1894 Broad Plain Boys Club has proudly existed but it has now been forced to change its name because the local council ruled it to be too sexist. Equally fatuously, maybe they were worried the boys didn't like being called plain and broad.

The club in Easton has now changed its name to 'Broad Plain working with young people group'. If the club didn't do this the council threatened to withdraw funding.

Spinsters and bachelors no longer to be married

[*The Times July 27 2005*]

The Government is to abolish the traditional terms 'spinster' and 'bachelor' in new reforms to marriage laws that will coincide with the introduction of gay weddings this year, *Times Online* has learnt.

Len Cook, the Registrar General, has decreed that marriage registers and certificates will no longer refer to newly-married couples in the late Middle English terminology. Instead, everyone tying the knot, whether gay or straight, will be designated as 'single'.

Divorced men and women are already denoted as such in marriage registers and on certificates. But those who have never been married are described as spinster and bachelor.

These terms will now disappear from England and Wales from December 5, when the change comes into effect. It is being made to bring marriage law into line with the new Civil Partnership Act, which becomes law on December 5, and which gives gay couples the right to legalise their relationship and enjoy the same tax benefits, pensions and property rights as married couples. The wealthier partner in a couple will also suffer the same financial penalties on 'divorce' or dissolution of the partnership.

Although it will be welcomed by those women who dislike the negative connotations of the term, the abolition of the word spinster will deepen the fears of bishops that the Government is set on undermining the institution of marriage as traditionally understood by the Church.

The Church of England, which refers to 'spinsters' and 'bachelors' of the parish when banns of marriage are read in church, is to come under pressure from the Registrar General's Office, part of the Office of National Statistics, to follow suit.

But the Church is firmly wedded to its spinsters and bachelors and the change is likely to generate a new Church–State dispute. A Church spokesman said: 'We are quite open to the way language is evolving, but we do not see any improvement being made here. This is something we will resist.

'The words bachelor and spinster have never been part of the wording of banns, but many clergy customarily use them and will no doubt continue to. As for registers, clergy merely fill these in according to the registrar's wishes, so changes in the registers are not something we would expect to influence.'

The wording of banns is not set in canon law and so a change would be easy to make.

A spokesman for the Registrar General's office said: 'The proposal is to make things consistent so civil marriage is the same as civil partnership. Men and women will be described as 'single' in both civil partnerships and civil registered weddings. There is no compulsion for clergy to do this but obviously we would prefer it if they did because it would be more consistent. We have not made the change yet. The likelihood is that it will come in on December 5 when civil partnerships become law. It is something that has been on the modernising agenda for civil registration for some time.'

Council bans 'brainstorming' and replaces the term with 'thought showers'... for fear of giving offence

[*Daily Mail June 20 2008*]

Brainstorming has undoubtedly generated some bolts of brilliance and flashes of inspiration over the years.

But in genteel Tunbridge Wells, the council decided it might lead to the traditionally Disgusted residents of the town becoming Offended as well.

So now the expression brainstorming has been banned. And in future, meetings to generate new ideas will be referred to as 'thought showers'.

Brainstorming, first coined in the 1890s, was used by psychiatrists to refer to severe nervous attacks. And although since the 1940s it has meant a meeting to produce new ideas, councillors are concerned it may prove offensive to epileptics.

The National Society for Epilepsy said this was unlikely. It surveyed members three years ago to ask whether they found the phrase offensive. Spokesman Amanda Cleaver said: 'The answer was a resounding No. It certainly wasn't deemed offensive at all. People thought it was a great word to describe the coming together and discussion of ideas.'

But diversity officers at Tunbridge Wells Borough Council are standing firm. Personnel chief Val Green said: 'We take equality and diversity issues very seriously. It is important to us not to offend people and we are sorry if through trying to avoid this, we have indeed caused offence to the very people we were trying not to offend.

'If the epilepsy association finds the term perfectly acceptable, then we welcome this clarification. If, however, the term does in fact offend even a small minority, we would encourage people to get in touch with us.'

'Thought shower' has already replaced 'brainstorming' elsewhere – including Redbridge Education Business Partnership in East London, the Deanes School in Essex, and the Church of England's Diocese of Southwark.

But critics remained unenthusiastic. Richard Colwill, of the mental health charity Sane, said. 'Using brainstorming in the context of a council meeting I wouldn't imagine would cause offence.'

Of the thought shower, he added: 'I don't think it will catch on.'

Christian honour is offensive
[*The Times May 8 2009*]
An honour established by the Queen 40 years ago has been declared unlawful after Muslims and Hindus complained that its Christian name and cross insignia were offensive.

The Trinity Cross of the Order of Trinity was established to recognise distinguished service and gallantry in the former colony of Trinidad and Tobago. It has been awarded to 62 people, including cricketers Garfield Sobers and Brian Lara, the novelist V.S. Naipaul and many of the islands' leading politicians and diplomats.

The Privy Council in London has ruled that the decoration is unconstitutional because it discriminates against non-Christians. Five British law lords said the creation of the honour breached the right to equality and the right to freedom of conscience and belief. The implications of the ruling on British decorations are being studied by lawyers at the Cabinet Office, which oversees the honours system. A spokesman said: 'We have noted the judgement and are monitoring the situation.'

The editor-in-chief of *Burke's Peerage and Gentry* said that changing the names of titles to remove their Christian references would destroy hundreds of years of history. 'Part of the significance of an honour is its antiquity and I can see no reason why they should be changed,' he said.

Public sector to ditch jargon to help people during the recession

[*Local Government Association media release March 18 2009*]
Council leaders have today published a list of 200 words that public bodies should not use if they want to communicate effectively with local people.

The Local Government Association list, which has been sent to councils across the country, sets out 200 words and phrases that all public sector bodies should avoid when talking to people about the work they do and the services they provide.

Words included on the list include:

taxonomy
re-baselining
mainstreaming
holistic governance

contestability
predictors of beaconicity
synergies

Council leaders have highlighted the fact that unless everyone who works in public services talks to people in a language that they can understand then the work they do becomes inaccessible. It also reduces the chances of people getting help during the recession.

Chairman of the Local Government Association, Cllr Margaret Eaton, said:

'The public sector must not hide behind impenetrable jargon and phrases. Why do we have to have 'coterminous, stakeholder engagement' when we could just 'talk to people' instead?

'During the recession, it is vital that we explain to people in plain English how to get access to the eight hundred different services that local government provides with taxpayers' money.

'Councils have a duty, not only to provide value for money to local people, but also to tell people what they get for the tax they pay. People would be furious if they have no idea of what services their cash is paying for and how they should get to use them.

'From claiming council tax benefit and how older people can get a lift to the shops, to telling people how they can get their old fridges picked up or how to report criminals who fly tip, people need to know what is available to them.

'Unless information is given to people to explain what help they can get during a recession then it could well lead to more people ending up homeless or bankrupt. If a council fails to explain what it does in plain English then local people will fail to understand its relevance to them or why they should bother to turn out and vote.

'We do not pretend to be perfect, but as this list shows, we are striving to make sure that people get the chance to understand what services we provide.'

A small selection of words and their alternatives

Across-the-piece – everyone working together
Actioned – done
Baseline – starting point
Challenge – problem
Champion – best
Citizen empowerment – people power
Client – person
Direction of travel – way forward
Distorts spending priorities – ignores people's needs
Income streams – money/cash
Lowlights – worst bits
Potentialities – chances
Resource allocation – money going to the right place
Revenue streams – money
Upward trend – getting better

According to the *Worcester Evening News* Wyre Forest District Council told new members of the council not to say, 'Ship-shape and Bristol fashion' or 'nitty gritty' as these were potentially racist phrases.

'Ship-shape and Bristol fashion' was said to be a derogatory description of black people who were ready for sale as slaves but this is completely wrong. The phrase more likely refers to the way wooden boats had to be constructed if they were not to be badly damaged when settling on the tidal harbourside in Bristol in the days before Bristol's Floating Harbour was created. An alternative version is that tackle and anything moveable had to be tightly secured to stop damage when the boat settled. No one is quite sure which is the original meaning.

Librarians redubbed 'audience development officers'

In January 2009 came the news that Edinburgh librarians were 'seething' after the powers that be decided they should henceforth be known as 'audience development officers' as part of a plan to drag libraries kicking and screaming 'into the 21st century'.

That's how the Caledonian edition of *The Sun* describes the move by 'barmy' council bosses, which prompted one irate 'book-stamper' to offer the obligatory: 'It is just political correctness gone daft. No one can see the point of this. The public will still call a librarian a librarian. It is idiotic.'

The change of job title was prompted by the decision to deploy 'self-service borrowing systems similar to those found at supermarket checkouts'. Up to 40 librarians could be for the off, and those who do hold onto their jobs will be expected to 'run computer courses, hold talks and encourage kids to read'. Accordingly, the council reckons the reinvented librarian is best described by the shiny new term which better reflects 'the extra responsibilities and more hands-on role of modern-day librarians'.

Sadly for the council, a union poll saw 95 per cent of workers reject the proposed changes. The opposing sides will meet for 'crunch talks' today amid the threat of industrial action.

A council spokesman assured: 'There will always be an appropriate level of staffing in libraries. Any staff freed up by self-service will be used across an expanded, more customer-friendly library service for Edinburgh.'

We're only doing it for your sake... to avoid a compensation Claim

Perhaps no single subject has outraged journalists and pundits the length and breadth of the UK quite as much as the dreaded 'Elf and Safety'. Almost every day there's another story about legislation designed to make sure we don't hurt ourselves, or others through sheer ignorance. And if you believe the small print, our ignorance knows no bounds.

It seems local authorities and those behind any kind of public event are so confused about regulations, they continue to request risk assessments for anything that can be assessed. According to the *Daily Telegraph*, an organ grinder from Derbyshire, popular at village fêtes, was told his act with a stuffed monkey had to be suspended until a risk assessment on the battery-operated ape had been carried out.

But again, we're going to defend the legislators: it's not really their fault, they're just afraid of being sued (and remember, most of the time compensation claims will come out of the public pot – it's you and me who end up paying). And they're right to be afraid. There was a case, in America, of a motor vehicle manufacturer being sued after a driver had a nasty accident in a camper van with an automatic gearbox. Assuming that 'automatic' meant the vehicle would look after itself, the driver had got it going along the freeway at 50 miles an hour, and then wandered into the living compartment to make herself a cup of coffee. The inevitable, inevitably, happened.

Weeks later, having recovered sufficiently from her injuries to consider how she could turn the accident to her advantage, the driver took the manufacturers to court on the grounds that at no point was it specified in the handbook that the driver was supposed to keep their hands on the steering wheel while the vehicle was in motion. And she won.

Need rescuing? Hang on a mo, I'll just fill in a form first...

[*Daily Mail January 20 2009*]

Coastguards have been ordered to fill in a health and safety questionnaire before they can respond to calls for help.

All 400 of Britain's rescue units have been told that before they travel to an accident scene they must complete a 'vehicle pre-journey risk assessment'.

It is feared lives may be lost as vital minutes could be taken up completing the forms as rescuers are preparing to respond to emergency call-outs.

Under the new rules, the teams have to take the time to answer four questions on the type of rescue and journey they are about to undertake.

Time's up for the old clockwinder

[*Daily Mail August 14 2008*]

Every week for the past 150 years, David R and his ancestors have wound the local market clock. But now council officials have called time on the practice – because they say it might cause an injury.

Mr R, 68, is the fifth generation of his family to keep the clock ticking in the market town of Llandover, Carmarthenshire.

He said the council is destroying a beloved local ritual. 'The council just told me not to do it any more – because their health and safety officers said I didn't tick any of their boxes,' he said.

Letter in *The Times*, January 28 2009

'Sir – For about 150 years we have managed to be told that the next train will be 'on' platform so-and-so without jumping onto the track to avoid being mown down. London Underground has now decided to announce that its trains will 'depart from alongside' the platform. How stupid do they think we are?'

Sparkler ban due to 'health and safety'

[*Tameside Advertiser October 25 2006*]

Town hall chiefs have denied being killjoys after they banned sparklers from Bonfire Night celebrations.

Families going to the Richmond Street fair and firework display in Ashton have been told the children's favourite is prohibited. The council says health and safety considerations have forced the ban.

A sparkler can reach temperatures of 1,000 degrees centigrade. Dozens of people are injured every year by hand-held fireworks.

But parents have reacted with disbelief to the ban, saying they alone should be responsible for their children's safety. Dad-of-two Michael W said: 'It's a disgrace and yet another example of the nanny state. It's part of the tradition.' Angela N, of Ashton, said: 'I think it's a little over the top. I'd let my son Scott, 10, play with sparklers as long as he was wearing gloves.'

Mum-of-three Caroline M, 32, of Hyde, said: 'In my opinion, it's an over-zealous decision by the council. I always have sparklers for my kids and it should be the parents who make sure they're handled safely.'

Hazel L, a grandmother-of-four, said: 'I think the ban is a good idea. If the trouble-causers decide to start throwing lit sparklers around, someone could be seriously hurt.'

Ashton town manager Robert Wheeler said: 'We do not want to spoil the enjoyment and fun of children and families attending the fireworks display.

'We are acting on guidance from the Health and Safety Executive and The Royal Society for the Prevention of Accidents (RoSPA) who advise organisers not to allow the use of sparklers at public displays.

'We do not wish to compromise safety at an event which we expect will attract up to 12,000 people.'

Icy New Year swim left out in the cold

[*Daily Mail January 1 2009*]

Each January swimmers have braved the icy waters of a reservoir to race for a wooden trophy and raise money for charity.

But organisers have called off the event in Todmorden, West Yorkshire, after failing to obtain insurance. They said firms were reluctant to cover one-off events for fear of heavy compensation claims.

Health and safety zealots ban toys in surgeries

[*Daily Express November 8 2008*]

Waiting-room toys have been banned from doctors' surgeries because health and safety zealots claim they could spread infection among children.

The move by a primary care trust was described by doctors and parents as 'bureaucracy gone mad'. One father who took his toddler son to see a doctor was shocked to find that toys had been withdrawn.

Martin R, who went to a health centre in Old Trafford, Manchester, with his son Oscar, three, said: 'There were no toys in the waiting room. It seems to have been decided without consulting the people it affects. We have been to St Mary's Hospital in Manchester recently and they make a good selection of toys available. They even have play co-ordinators, so we cannot understand why Trafford are taking such an approach.'

Health and safety killjoys ban flowers and get–well cards in hospital ... because they clutter up wards

[*This is Bristol August 13 2008*]

The 'get well soon' card has long been accepted as a way of cheering up a loved one stuck in hospital.

John N sent one to his Aunt Edna as she recovered after a fall and expected to see it beside her bed when he visited. To his surprise, however, there was no sign of it or of any other cards on the ward. When he asked his elderly aunt why, she told him she had sent the card home because staff had forbidden her from putting it up by her bedside in order to keep the area free of clutter for the cleaners.

Mr N said: 'We wanted to cheer her up and there aren't many things you can give to someone who is ill. I thought it was taking away something very important from someone who wasn't very well. If I was on a ward, I'd like to receive cards.'

He had earlier been stopped by a senior nurse at Frenchay Hospital in Bristol from taking in flowers for his aunt because plants were banned 'for health and danger reasons'. 'We had never heard of this before and can only assume it is due to any bugs in the flowers or vases being knocked over,' said Mr N, a 73-year-old retired fund-raiser from Brislington, near Bristol.

'We asked if they could be left in a dayroom or nurses' quarters but this was also rejected and they wouldn't dispose of them so the alternative was to bin them or bring them home.'

Mr N added: 'Frenchay is a wonderful hospital but it seems a shame people can't receive cards or flowers. They could maybe put the cards and flowers in an area away from the beds.'

His aunt, who is in her nineties, is recovering at home in Bristol.

Hospital bosses said senior nurses would ask for cards to be moved if they were taking up too much space and said flowers were discouraged because they could clutter lockers and hamper cleaning.

But Kate Jopling, of Help The Aged, said: 'Many older people find get well cards to be a reassuring and pleasant distraction from illness while in hospital.

'While we fully understand the paramount importance of keeping hospital wards clean and tidy we can't help wondering whether this isn't a case of using a sledgehammer to crack a nut.

'We would hope that with a bit of flexible thinking it would be possible to allow older people to recover with appropriate support from family and friends.'

Richard Cottle, of North Bristol NHS Trust, which runs Frenchay Hospital, said: 'We don't prevent patients displaying get well cards on the wards. However, maintaining a clean environment and reducing infection is this trust's number one priority.

'It is particularly important that the area around the patient's bed is kept as clean as possible and is free of clutter so our cleaners can get complete access.

'Responsibility for cleanliness lies with the sister-in-charge on each ward and if they feel cards on display by a patient's bedside are getting in the way of domestic staff, they will ask them to be taken down.

'We hope this particular patient and their family understand the very good reasons why they were asked to do this.'

Earlier this year, parents visiting Birmingham's Children's Hospital were advised to bring new soft toys in factory-sealed boxes to prevent the spread of superbugs.

The guidance stemmed from concerns that toy fabric is a breeding ground for MRSA and Clostridium difficile.

PC publishers ban dragon from breathing fire in children's book...

[*Daily Mail November 11 2007*]

A leading children's author was told to drop a fire-breathing dragon shown in a new book – because the publishers feared they could be sued under health and safety regulations.

It is just one of the politically correct cuts Lindsey Gardiner says she has been told to make in case youngsters act out the stories. As well as the scene showing her dragon toasting marshmallows with his breath, illustrations of an electric cooker with one element glowing red and of a boy on a ladder have had to go.

Ms Gardiner, 36, who has written and illustrated 15 internationally successful children's books, featuring her popular characters Lola, Poppy and Max, says such editing decisions are now common.

Teenage cleaner told: Don't do the vacuuming, it's too dangerous

[*Western Daily Press October 24 2008*]

Bosses at a cleaning firm have threatened a 16-year-old with the sack because they say he is too young to use a vacuum cleaner.

Hardworking student Karl W was employed by Apollo Cleaning to work at offices near his home in Chippenham.

However, the teenager was stunned when, a week into his new job, bosses banned him from using the vacuum cleaner on health and safety grounds.

They claimed it was not safe for Karl to start using the equipment until he was 18, as they feared he may injure himself.

There are any number of stories about people not being allowed on buses because they were carrying items deemed to be a threat to the health and safety of other passengers. More often than not, paint is to blame. We rather liked this story because of the reaction of the banned passenger, a pensioner who, after her altercation with the driver, simply put the paint in a carrier bag, waited ten minutes and got on the next bus.

Pensioner with tub of paint refused bus travel

[Lancashire Telegraph February 20 2008]

Seventy-six-year-old Breda F got the brush off as she tried to take a sealed two-and-a-half-litre tub of paint on the bus.

Baffled Breda was left 'upset and embarrassed' when the driver put the brakes on her ten-minute trip home. The great grandmother was told she was not allowed on with her £2.49 tub of emulsion – because it was potentially dangerous.

Ironically she waited ten minutes for the next bus, concealed the tub in a carrier bag with a bag of bulbs and got on without any problems.

The incident certainly got the Irish widow's paddy up. 'I said to the driver, you what, are you joking?' she said. 'But he just said: "you are not allowed on with that."

'He even said: "it's flammable stuff."

'I said: "it's emulsion," and he said: "I don't care, you still can't get on".' A spokesman for Stagecoach said: 'In the past we have had problems where customers have brought on paint. The bus has been in transit and it has come open spilling paint all over the floor and onto customers.'

Sorry, we can't welcome you home

Family and friends pulled out all the stops to welcome a wounded paratrooper home from Iraq. They festooned his home with yellow ribbons, balloons, banners and bunting. Sadly, highway officials in Doncaster, South Yorkshire, ordered that the bunting that stretched high across the road be taken down because it constituted a safety hazard.

Policemen banned from riding bikes...

[*Daily Mail November 22 2007*]

Police officers must pass a cycling proficiency test before they are allowed to patrol the streets on their bikes. They have been told to walk, drive, or use public transport until they succeed. But the decision by Cheshire Police has been described as 'health and safety gone mad'. Officers were given mountain bikes earlier this year and the patrols proved popular with the public because they act as a visible deterrent. The cycles allow officers to cover a wide area and they can reach places where police cars cannot get to. Officers on mountain bikes can chase criminals down narrow lanes and through parks.

But in September, a Police Community Support Officer had died while on a mountain bike patrol. The 21-year-old, who served with the neighbouring Greater Manchester force, suffered massive head injuries after being hit by a lorry in Wigan. As a result, Greater Manchester Police banned hundreds of officers who had been on cycle patrols for less than a year from riding bikes. They will be allowed back on their bikes only when their skills have been properly assessed. The Cheshire force has followed suit and decided that PCSOs and officers who patrol on mountain bikes should take a proficiency test. The chairman of Alderley Edge Parish Council, in Cheshire, was unhappy about Cheshire Police's decision: 'All PCSOs were told they had to do cycling proficiency tests and until they had passed them, they had to either cadge a lift to work or use public transport. It is unbelievable to think that the PCSOs are going around schools giving advice to children on cycling proficiency and road safety and they're not even allowed to ride their bikes themselves. It's health and safety gone mad.'

Don't sit down unless you know how

Firefighters were not allowed to take a rest in between call-outs on their new, £400 reclining chair until they'd been trained to do so. Greater Manchester Fire Service went to the trouble of producing a four-page safety manual containing full instructions on how to sit on the chair to make sure there were no accidents.

Picturesque pond – or water hazard?

Health and safety worries prompted a parish council to decide that a pond in the picturesque village of West Itchenor, West Sussex was no longer a pretty habitat for ducks and fish, but a 'water hazard', which should be fenced and fitted with a sign warning of deep water. While the councillors felt they had to act as they were liable for any accidents, local residents were less than impressed. One said: 'As far as I know the pond has a good accident record in that nobody has been hurt there. It's more of a muddy puddle than a big open pond.'

Poppy Pins

Have you noticed how the poppies sold to commemorate Remembrance Day no longer come with pins? Ever wondered why? Yep, it's all down to good old Health and Safety fears. The Royal British Legion has become concerned wearers may sue if they are injured by the pins and has been phasing them out. To be honest the new, longer-stemmed poppies are easier to wear, so maybe this one isn't such a bad thing.

Army's Bagpipers and Drummers Must Play Safe and Use Earplugs

[*The Times July 4 2006*]

Army bagpipers are to wear earplugs because of fears that the military might be sued by soldiers who claim that their hearing has been damaged by excessive noise. Pipers are also to be banned from practising for more than 24 minutes a day outside, and 15 minutes indoors.

The pipes are famous for terrifying the enemy, but new army guidelines, based on a study carried out by the Army Medical Directorate Environmental Health Team, say that pipers should wear earplugs to protect themselves from hearing loss. The guidelines also apply to drummers.

Piping experts and military veterans have criticised the rules as typical of the health and safety culture of today's 'cotton wool Army'. However, a spokeswoman for the Army in Scotland said the new rules showed that it was serious about protecting soldiers.

The Armed Forces lost their traditional exemption from health and safety legislation in 2000, although that does not apply when the forces are on active service.

A few more daft safety regulations...

Carpenters and other woodworkers are reputedly told by the Health and Safety Executive not to use brooms to sweep up sawdust because they are considered dangerous.

Musicians at the BBC Proms told to play more quietly to avoid breaching health and safety regulations.

The pulpit in an 800-year old Dorset church falls victim to health and safety rules. Inspectors say preacher might injure himself while climbing the seven steps. ['Lord Protect Us!' said *The Mail on Sunday* August 10 2008]

Incredibly a mother was reportedly stopped from breast-feeding her 11-week-old baby in a swimming pool, as it breached a leisure centre's poolside ban on food and drink.

The 26-year-old mum was left fuming when a member of staff told her she could not feed her baby by the pool at a Nottingham leisure centre. The city council has since apologised, promising new guidelines for pool staff.

Massive bill to raise 'too low' park benches by three inches

[*Daily Mail June 2 2007*]

Park benches across the country will have to be replaced at a cost of hundreds of thousands of pounds – because they are too low.

Under new health and safety laws, benches must be more than 17.75 inches high so the elderly and disabled can get off them easily.

The new rules came to light after Bramcote Crematorium in Nottinghamshire was told by officials from the local Broxtowe council to replace 40 memorial benches costing £400 each. An inspector found that the benches were 14.75 inches high – three inches lower than the 'allowed minimum' height and five inches lower than the 'optimum' height.

The crematorium has also been ordered to pay a further £200,000 for lighting, because, under the same legislation, the new benches must be lit at night.

The crematorium's manager, said: 'The inspector went around with a tape measure measuring everything for compliance with the Disability Discrimination Act 2005.

'Apparently, it means that the buttocks of infirm people are below the point at which they can easily return to a standing position, and 72 per cent of our visitors are elderly.

'But we also have to pay to put the new benches on an elevated slab, clear enough space at the side to give wheelchair access and make sure all the benches across our 18-acre site are properly lit. This will have staggering financial implications for us – about £200,000 – and we have to carry it out within two years.

'It is very difficult to strike a balance between our responsibility to the bereaved and the other obligations placed on us.'

To underline the nonsense of all this, the order has led to the benches – many of which were paid for by bereaved families in memory of their loved ones – being removed.

BBC wheel nuts

Two BBC radio presenters had to be watched by two first-aid volunteers as they took turns to change a car wheel. The corporation called in the St. John's Ambulancemen under health and safety rules for a programme about learning new skills at BBC Radio Essex's car park in Chelmsford.

Four-inch doorstep is dangerous

Hospital transport staff at City Hospital, Birmingham, refused to take a 98-year-old home after deciding that her four-inch doorstep was a safety risk. (*Daily Mail* January 2008). The decision was reversed when the story made the headlines.

Starbuck water scandal

[*The Sun October 6 2008*]

Starbucks was blasted by environmental experts last night after *The Sun* discovered it pours millions of litres of precious water down the drain at its coffee shops.

The giant coffee chain has a policy of keeping a tap running non-stop at all its 10,000 outlets worldwide, wasting **23.4 MILLION** litres a day.

That would provide enough daily water for the entire two million-strong population of drought-hit Namibia in Africa or fill an Olympic pool every 83 minutes.

Every Starbucks branch has a cold tap behind the counter providing water for a sink called a 'dipper well', used for washing spoons and utensils. Staff are banned from turning the water off under bizarre health and safety rules

– bosses claim a constant flow stops germs breeding in the taps.

Starbucks has built up a massive chain, popular with coffee drinkers from Hollywood stars to builders, and proudly boasts of its work for the environment. But water companies accused the firm of harming the environment by frittering away a vital natural resource.

And the claim that running taps are needed for hygiene reasons was dismissed by experts as 'nonsense'.

Starbucks has 698 branches in Britain, each open for 13 hours a day.

Ladder-less window cleaners

People given work as window cleaners are not allowed to use ladders due to health and safety concerns, claimed Nick Clegg, the Liberal Democrat leader on a visit to Bristol in April, 2009.

Mr Clegg learned of the rule at a Salvation Army building in the city.

The activity was designed to publicise how 'social enterprise companies' are finding work for the long-term jobless and homeless.

He said that he was surprised when a cleaner told him they could not use ladders because of the risk. Instead, they used a brush on a pole through which water was pumped. The politician took full use of the photo-opportunity to be seen satirically washing windows using the extended brush.

Stepladders are banned from Oxford's library

[*Daily Mail May 9 2009*]

Stepladders have been banned from part of Oxford University's historic Bodleian library – because of health and safety fears.

The ruling by officials means that students cannot use books on the higher shelves of the Duke Humfrey reading room. However, the university is standing its ground and refusing to move the books from their 'original historic location' on the room's balcony.

As a result of the stalemate, students have to travel to libraries as far away as London to view other copies. Art history student Kelsey, 21, had to travel 80 miles to London to view a copy of Arthur Johnston's 1637 work *Delitiae Poetarum Scotorum* after librarians refused to get it down for her. 'It's madness because I can practically see the Bodleian's copy every time I walk into Duke Humfrey's.'

Stepladders have been used by scholars to reach books since the library was built more than 400 years ago. But the University's Health and Safety Officer put his foot down and they were removed two weeks ago.

A notice given to students requesting the books reads: 'Unable to fetch book kept on top shelf in gallery. Due to new health and safety measures, stepladders can no longer be used.' The library's director of administration and finance, said: 'The balcony has a low rail and we have been instructed by the health and safety office that this increases the risk'.

Health and safety 'nonsense' riles BBC veteran

John Simpson has criticised the obsession with health and safety after being given a risk assessment form 'the size of a telephone directory' before filming the 'Top Dog' series.

The reporter, 64, said: 'I am the wrong age to care about that sort of stuff. I really hate all that nonsense.'

Rubber rings can spread germs

[*Metro July 2007*]

A council has banned its leisure centres from lending rubber rings and armbands to swimmers amid health and safety fears.

Blowing up the inflatables by mouth is considered too risky for spreading germs and unseen punctures might lead to an accident.

Bournemouth Borough Council in Dorset has imposed the ban following professional guidelines from The Institute of Sport and Recreation Management.

And we end this chapter with another uplifting story about risk-taking Health and Safety Officers. It's good to know that the spirit of rebellion is alive and well in Gloucestershire.

Health and Safety officers love danger

[*Western Daily Press January 7 2009*]

As health and safety officers, Roger Garbett and his Forest of Dean District Council colleagues should probably be more cautious than most when it comes to diving into sub-zero water.

But they enthusiastically took the plunge in the icy waters of a disused quarry. Dubbing themselves 'Health and Safety Gone Mad', they are on a mission to convince us the nanny state is not stopping us being adventurous.

Roger and fellow officers from the council's environmental health department Keith Leslie, Haydn Brookes and Rhys Thomas say they are fed-up taking the blame for bosses who do not want to put up Christmas decorations in the office or poor organisers who cannot be bothered to arrange a pancake race.

So they want to prove to people that they do not expect them to stay at home wrapped in cotton wool.

By day they make sure local eateries are clean, that factories and events conform to the regulations and prosecute those responsible for accidents.

But in their spare time they take part in activities ranging from bog snorkelling to chariot racing – and are even planning an Arctic expedition.

After hearing health and safety officials were blamed for ending a traditional Christmas Day swim in Southwold, Suffolk, Roger and Keith took a New Year dip at the national diving centre in Tidenham, near Chepstow, to prove to people they can still do it.

The Whackiest insurance
Claims

We've already touched on the fact that it is the fear of being sued for compensation that's behind the majority of the strangest bans and regulations. We like the story about the man who was planning to sue his local health trust because he hadn't died. When told he had a terminal illness and only months to live, he sold up everything for a great splurge. Around the time he was expected to die, he was given the bad news that he had been misdiagnosed and there was nothing seriously wrong with him.

Some people will phone their local branch of Nowin, Nofee Solicitors at the merest drop of a hat, or a pane of glass, or a hot drink. Or simply whack in an insurance claim. You don't believe us? Read on. Here is a hand-picked selection of remarkable insurance claims.

Insurers were faced with a bill for thousands of pounds after the theft of vibrators from a sex shop.

The adult toys, pinched from a store in Solihull, West Midlands, were never recovered and Lloyds TSB Insurance paid out.

The firm also revealed it had received claims from a man who alleged a magpie had stolen his glasses from the bedroom, and another from a couple who tried to recoup the cash for a bedpost broken during love-making.

Lloyds' Phil Loney said: 'I never cease to be intrigued by the claims made to us.'

Bizarre Christmas insurance claims

From *Money Mail*, December 17 2008
Candle mishaps and dozy dogs – that's why we claim at Christmas. Money Mail's James Salmon looks at some of the more bizarre Christmas insurance claims.

THE HUNGRY POOCH

Most of us over-indulge during the festive period, but six-year-old cocker spaniel Suki took it a step too far last year.

The pooch scoffed 12 mince pies while her owner's back was turned, including the foil and packaging.

Owner Amanda A says: 'I got home in the evening and she was lying on her back with her feet in the air. She was enormous – twice the size she usually is. I had to rush her to the emergency vet. She was sick all over my new car.' The vet said there was not much more he could do. She was told to buy pills the next day which would help Suki pass the foil, which risked puncturing her gut.

Care worker Amanda claimed for the cost of the pills and the trip to the vet – a total of £200. Unfortunately, the policy from More Than didn't cover the cost of cleaning her car.

TV DISASTER

Any families intending to buy a Nintendo Wii this Christmas should take heed of the accident that befell two youngsters insured by Home & Legacy.

While concentrating on a game, they threw the handset of their new Nintendo Wii through the equally new plasma-screen TV. This resulted in a £1,000 insurance claim for a replacement.

CHRISTMAS CANDLES
One man burned his house down, and somehow managed to claim £330,000 damage on his home insurance policy. He attached candles to his Christmas tree and left the room. Unsurprisingly, the tree caught fire before spreading to the rest of the house.

HOW STUPID CAN YOU GET?
'As I turned the ignition key, I glanced at my mother-in-law and headed over the embankment.'

'I opened the oven, armed with a baster and a pair of oven gloves, but the turkey was heavier than I expected and it flew out of the oven on to the floor. We had a lovely meal, but the carpet was ruined.'

'I got up on Christmas morning to make the Christmas dinner, only to see that the freezer had defrosted on its own.'

'I was on the way to the doctors with rear-end trouble when my universal joint gave way.'

'While moving furniture around for Christmas dinner, I tripped over the plug when carrying the TV set and dropped it in the fireplace.'

Dancing fish and decorating dogs: strange insurance claims

Working as a claims adviser for an insurance firm probably wouldn't rank on most people's list of exciting jobs. But occasionally a claim is lodged that brings a smile to even the most hardened insurance veteran.

Most people take out contents insurance to protect their possessions from the unexpected, such as theft or accidents. However, as a survey from Lloyds TSB Insurance shows, there are some accidents that are so unlikely as to be downright bizarre.

Here are six of the strangest claims received by the insurer last year, with his comments:

One claims adviser thought there was something fishy going on when he received a very unusual claim for a digital radio that took a surprise dip in the garden pond. It turned out that the policyholder's granddaughter had submerged the radio in the pond to 'play music to the fish to make them dance'. Wet Wet Wet eat your hearts out…

We've all heard of pool sharks, but what about pool fish? One wayward player overshot the pocket by such a long way that the cue ball bounced off the pool table and shattered a goldfish bowl on the table beyond. The name of the fish who, happily, survived the incident? Jaws. When questioned by police, he said he couldn't remember what had happened…

Many people are extremely scornful of modern art, so no doubt the next unusual claim will raise a smile. A Labrador left home alone by its owners brushed his tail into a discarded painting tray and proceeded to wag white emulsion all over the living room carpet, sofa and walls. Maybe Jackson Pollock wasn't such a genius after all.

Speed cameras are the scourge of many a motorist, so some of us may have some sympathy with one unlucky claimant. Fed up with being consistently snapped by a Gatso near his home, he decided one night to exact his own revenge by crushing the offending spying eye. However, he hadn't bargained on the sturdiness of the lamp post it was attached to and proceeded to write off his motor. Though he still claims it was an accident, somehow I doubt his claims adviser believes him.

Everyone has a barbecue disaster story, but our next strange case makes the salmonella-inducing undercooked chicken I 'treated' my friends to seem a mere laughing matter. During last year's heatwave, one enthusiastic host decided to use a disposable BBQ on his roof terrace. It was all going to plan until he caught a whiff of something burning that definitely wasn't sausages. On removing the BBQ from his asphalt roof, he discovered that the red-hot coals had burned a hole right through into the room below.

Mirror, signal, manoeuvre… I'm sure there's something I've forgotten. Our final foolish claimant loaded bags into the back seat of his car after visiting a friend and proceeded to drive home. He reached his driveway unscathed and was backing in when he heard the horrible sound of crunching metal. Only then did he realise that he had left both back doors of his car wide open throughout the course of his 10-minute drive home.

It's not unusual for motor insurance companies to receive claims that are obviously a little exaggerated and possibly even made up, but when Norwich Union put together a list of the most bizarre claims it received last year, we couldn't have made it up for ourselves!

Most freak accidents are caused by animals of one type or another and not just your average household cat or dog running across a road, either; squirrels, zebras, cows and even wasps all feature in the top ten list of bizarre claims.

Items of food are the second biggest cause of unusual car insurance claims and though vegetables lodging themselves under your brake pedal is a very serious matter, we couldn't help but snigger when we heard about the escape of the frozen kebab...

In tenth spot: 'As I came over a hill, I hit a cow in the middle of the road, which then hit the bonnet and shattered the windscreen with its rear end.' Before we go any further it should be noted that the cow involved in this incident actually survived the ordeal. Something tells me though that the car may not have. Hitting a large animal, be it a cow or deer, is always going to be a traumatic experience (for driver and animal alike), but the resulting damage will write most cars off.

Another cow is implicated in ninth place, with the simple but effective 'A cow jumped on my quad bike'. If you're a fan of Gary Larson cartoons you'll already have an image in your head of the cow speeding off into the sunset on some hapless human's quad-bike, with a little red helmet bouncing up and down on his head! What is unclear though is whether the claim was for theft or accidental damage. After all, how many cows do you know that can drive a quad-bike competently?

Number eight on the list involves yet another cow, though this time the male of the species: 'My parked car was hit by a bull which had escaped from an agricultural show'. If the car really was parked, as the insured claimed, then it is likely that the call centres of several insurers were buzzing with this one and the traditional catchphrase 'bull in a china shop' could have been changed forever to the far more expensive contents of an agricultural show car park.

Food starts causing trouble at number seven on the list with nothing more troublesome than your common garden potato. However, as the claim stated: 'I couldn't brake because a potato was lodged behind the brake'. This innocent-looking root vegetable can cause a nasty accident. No doubt the driver thought that the shopping was stowed away safely, but this evil potato found a way out, and then cunningly burrowed under the driver's seat, between the driver's legs and next thing you know you're apologising to the guy in front for rear-ending him. Could happen to anyone. I'm surprised we haven't heard of a supermarket chain being sued for insubstantially secured shopping bags.

Picture number six happening and you have to admit it's a funny image: 'While I was waiting at traffic lights, a wasp went down my trouser leg which made me hit the accelerator and prang the car in front'. That's straight out of a Chevy Chase movie, though in his case the driver in front would be a big and angry body builder. I don't know about you, but given the choice of a wasp down my trousers or a little 'discussion' with a human out-house, I think I'd take my chances that the latter can see the funny side of things.

In fifth place: 'A zebra collided with my car when I was at a safari park'. Ah come on, a zebra can't just collide with a car by mistake! They're not like shopping trolleys after all, and most animals will do their best to get away from a car full of people. This has to be one of those claims the insurance company knows not to be true, yet can't exactly question the guilty party.

Those troublesome herbivores are back in action in fourth place: 'A herd of cows licked my car and caused damage to the paintwork'. You learn something new every day; apparently a cow's tongue is rough enough to scratch the normally strong surface of a car's paintwork. Did they think it was a big cow lollipop or something? No prizes for guessing the colour of the car.

Though only number three on Norwich Union's list, this is my personal favourite: 'As I was driving round a bend, when one of the doors opened and a frozen kebab flew out, hitting and damaging a passing car'. Dodgy grammar aside, that claim raises more eyebrows than the average *Carry On* movie. First of all, how did the door just open? Secondly, what on earth is a frozen kebab?

Number two: 'The car was parked when a reindeer fell on the bonnet of my car'. I know that this probably happened in another safari park, though again the animal is not very likely to be at fault, but am I the only one to have pictured one of Rudolf the Red-Nosed Reindeer's friends kicking the bucket mid-air and tumbling down onto the unfortunate claimant's bonnet?

Finally, the winning claim is 'A frozen squirrel fell out of a tree and crashed through the windscreen on to the passenger seat'. What's with the frozen items? Very suspect. Must have been a cold winter.

in the courts

Top Bunk Trouble

A prisoner who hurt his head when he rolled out of bed while asleep in his cell sued the jail for compensation. He claimed that convicts' beds were 'an accident waiting to happen.'

Caretaker sues school for £50,000 after fall because he 'was not trained how to use stepladder'

The *Daily Mail* had this incredible story in June 2008:

A school caretaker injured falling off a stepladder is seeking up to £50,000 damages – because he 'was not trained to use it'.

He admitted to a court he had used stepladders for at least 30 years in his previous job as a petrol station owner.

But he claims the accident with the six-foot ladder would not have happened if he had received the right training.

The 73-year-old fell while removing cards and staples from a gym wall at a primary school, near Romsey in Hampshire, in January 2004.

He fractured his skull, broke a cheekbone, split a kidney and spent time in intensive care at Southampton General Hospital, Winchester County Court heard.

He is suing Hampshire County Council for liability, claiming his bosses did not train him properly.

Mr G who is married, says he was never told it was unsafe to place the ladder side-on to the wall he was working on

– the position it was in when he fell. He is claiming damages of at least £15,000 and up to £50,000. Hampshire County Council denies negligence.

He said that when he started at the school in October 2002 he received induction training from a caretaker support officer.

He admitted he had ticked boxes on a form to say he had been trained on ladder safety, but added: 'When you are given something to sign by your superior you just sign it. I signed to say I had ladder training but the extent of that was not to stand on the top step and not to go above three metres.'

Mr G says he didn't receive training to climb a stepladder similar to this one. 'I thought that was the extent of ladder training. I didn't know there were other things regarding ladders.'

He denied he was standing on the top step when he fell. However, the court heard he told police officers called to the scene that he had been on the top platform and that he blamed himself.

He countered: 'I don't remember what I said. I was dazed. But I wasn't on the top step because I had no need to go to the top step.'

The caretaker support officer told the court she had instructed Mr G about the hazards. He was also given a detailed manual on all aspects of his job.

In a defence statement, the council said the caretaker was negligent and 'knew perfectly well how to use a stepladder'.

When asked by the judge if he had a stepladder at home, Mr G said that he did.

What a thong and dance: Woman sues Victoria's Secret over G-string injury

[*Daily Mail June 18 2008*]

A woman is taking legal action against world-famous lingerie label Victoria's Secret after sustaining an eye injury while trying on a thong.

The incident occurred, says the Los Angeles woman, as she was putting on a decorative low-rise 'v-string', Victoria's Secret's own version of the g-string, from the 'Sexy Little Thing' line.

According to a lawsuit filed last week in Los Angeles Superior Court, Macrida Patterson, 52, alleges that a piece of metallic embellishment that should have been stitched firmly onto the garment flew off and hit her in the eye.

Her lawyer told an investigative website a 'design problem' caused the decorative piece to come loose and strike his client in the eye, causing damage to her cornea.

He added the eye injury, which caused her to miss a few days of work as a traffic officer with the LA Department of Transportation, will be 'affecting her the rest of her life'.

Victoria's Secret is famous for its glamorous fashion shows starring the likes of supermodels Giselle, Heidi Klum and Tyra Banks.

No Christmas joy

Vicar who refused to sing 'O Little Town of Bethlehem'

[*Daily Mail December 12 2008*]

A vicar has banned the Christmas carol 'O Little Town of Bethlehem' from his services after witnessing the strife-torn state of Jesus's birthplace.

He has decided that the words 'How still we see thee lie' are too far removed from the reality of Bethlehem today and should not be sung in his parish.

At his district council's civic carol service, the vicar told the congregation he could not join in the singing of the carol.

Christmas cheer ordered to stop

[*The Times December 10 2008*]

A lollipop man has been ordered to remove silver tinsel from his sign.

45-year-old Kevin S decorated his placard to spread Christmas cheer, but after receiving an anonymous complaint, officials at Hampshire County Council instructed him to take it off in case it distracted motorists.

Mr S said: 'When I was told the tinsel had to go I was in tears and so were the children'.

Angels' wings are fire risk

Devon teachers have banned primary school kids from wearing angel wings in their nativity. They fear pupils carrying candles in the play could set their festive costumes on fire. Headmistress Linda M told *The Sun* (Christmas 2007) the school had made the decision after a risk assessment. 'You have to be so careful these days. If the children are carrying candles there's a danger if they turn suddenly.'

Mrs M of the school in Paignton added that in the previous year's nativity play pupils had suffered scratches from the wings. The wings were made from cardboard and flammable material. The other teachers agreed it was sensible not to have wings.

But one mum spoke for many when she said her daughter would be upset by the ban. 'I think it's awful,' said Mandy. 'How can they expect the children to look the part without wings? It all seems over the top to me.'

Christmas is axed in Oxford

Council leaders in Oxford have decided to ban the word Christmas from this year's festive celebrations to make them more 'inclusive'.

But the decision to rename the series of events the 'Winter Light Festival' has been criticised by religious leaders and locals said it was ludicrous.

Christmas puddings can choke you

Traditional Christmas puddings are to go on sale in a supermarket with sixpence coins attached separately, reported the *Daily Mail* in November 2005.

Sainsbury's carried out a nationwide search for the old 6d coins in order to revive the tradition. But unlike puddings sold in Victorian times, the chain's puddings are health-and-safety protected.

'The coins were traditionally hidden in the pudding mixture and brought good luck to whoever found them. Just 9,000 of the puddings sold at Sainsbury's with coins attached will go on sale for £10 each.' Most of the coins used date from 1957, said the store. Some sixpences can sell for as much as £45 to dealers.

Spokeswoman Claire Goldhill said, 'we can't supply the coin already mixed into the pudding because it presents a choking hazard. We have provided a collector's card that you can place under a mystery plate or table mat for one lucky friend or family member to find.'

The traditional pudding contains a mixture of fruit and nuts [what about allergies?], along with champagne, sherry and cognac. It is presented in a traditional ceramic bowl topped with a linen covering called a mop cap.

Festive lollipop lady is unsafe
[*Daily Telegraph December 13 2007*]
A lollipop lady has been banned from wearing festive fancy dress because of safety fears.

Popular Margaret R, 54, has delighted pupils, parents and motorists in Southampton for two decades as she collects for charity.

But after a complaint by two parents, the city council said she could not take children across the road unless she wore her reflective coat.

Mrs R, a grandmother who is collecting for the Mayor of Southampton's appeal fund, said: 'I was pretty cheesed off when they told me because I'd spent a lot of time and effort on this year's costume. Why am I suddenly a health and safety risk? When they used the expression I thought they were saying 'elf and safety' for a joke.'

Over the years the lollipop lady has raised thousands of pounds but is not expecting much this year in her normal uniform.

She added: 'I can see the council's point but it makes you think why now after I've been doing this for 20 years. It just seems daft.'

A council spokesman said: 'If a crossing patrol supervisor does not wear a reflective jacket they are not insured and if hit, the motorist could not be prosecuted.'

Last night, however, a mother hit back at the decision. Sandy McC said: 'It's absolutely terrible.

'We've been living here for about 10 years and she's made a new costume every year.'

One councillor said: 'It seems these days that the council is frightened of people suing them. If nothing has happened over the years why would it happen now?'

Politically correct Christmas carols drop 'king', 'son' and 'virgin'

[*Daily Telegraph December 12 2008*]
Churches are making traditional Christmas carols politically correct by removing words such as king, son and virgin, it is claimed.

Enduring favourites such as 'Hark the Herald Angels Sing' and 'God Rest Ye Merry, Gentlemen' are being altered by clergy to make them more 'modern and inclusive'.

But churchgoers say there is no need to change the popular carols and complain that the result is a 'festive car crash' if not everyone is singing from the same hymn sheet.

It comes just a day after a Church of England vicar banned his congregation from singing 'O Little Town of Bethlehem' because he believed its words do not reflect the suffering endured by modern residents of Jesus's birthplace.

Another clergyman has rewritten 'The Twelve Days of Christmas' to include Aids victims, drug addicts and hoodies.

Steve Goddard, co-editor of the Christian website Ship of Fools, which is running a competition to find the worst example of a rewritten carol, said: 'It's a festive car crash.

'Half the congregation sing familiar words from memory, while the rest stumble over revised alternatives. Our readers are telling us straight – for some new versions there should be no room at the inn.'

Included in the 'theologically-modified, politically-corrected' carols encountered by visitors to the website are 'Hark the Herald Angels Sing' in which the line 'Glory to the newborn King' has been replaced by 'Glory to the Christ child, bring'.

The well-known refrain of ' Come All Ye Faithful – O come let us adore Him' – has also been changed in one church to 'come in adoration', both changes apparently made for fear the original was sexist.

Santa slapped with health and safety ban
[*Metro November 29 2007*]
Santa Claus has been banned from riding his sleigh on his visits to a market town because of health and safety fears.

For the last 30 years, Father Christmas has been pulled round Alnwick and villages surrounding the historic Northumberland town on a trailer owned by the district council.

The Alnwick Lions charity fundraisers organised the festive visits, but an insurance wrangle has put a block on Santa's pre-Christmas visits this year. An Alnwick District Council spokeswoman said: 'Our insurance company has told us that our insurance would not be valid as the Alnwick Lions' use would not be classed as part of our core business.

'We always try to help with community projects, but regrettably, this is out of our hands.'

Graham Luke, of Alnwick Lions, told the *Northumberland Gazette*: 'It is health and safety. We have become Americanised – that's the best way of putting it. It is very frustrating because it is a tradition that has been going on for so long.'

But children in the area will not miss out on the festive spirit as a local firm has lent the Lions a bus to ferry Santa around, instead of the traditional sleigh.

God Rest Ye Merry People
[*Daily Mail December 23 2004*]
A choir was made to sing a politically correct Christmas Carol in Cardiff this Christmas. Instead of the traditional

carol lyrics 'God Rest Ye Merry Gentlemen', they were told to change the words to 'God Rest Ye Merry People'.

The change was ordered by the Dean of Llandaff Cathedral in Cardiff. The amended version was attacked as over-the-top political correctness by churchgoing Tory politician Glyn Davies, who said: 'This smacks to me of political correctness gone mad. I haven't heard this version but I would not consider singing it under any circumstances.'

Panto stars told: don't throw sweets

[*Daily Mirror December 7 2007*]

Oh No, you can't... throwing sweets to children is too perilous for panto, stars have been warned.

For soft-centred theatre chiefs are in meltdown after a legal warning they could be sued if a chocolate tossed from the stage hurts someone in the audience.

Theatre director Kevin Lynch said: 'It is a shame a tradition has ended but we have no choice – we have to make sure we do not open ourselves to being sued.

'In the past children have bumped heads jumping for sweets and you get a few tears from those who don't get them. But last year we had two pensioners complain they had been hit and, for them, the performance was spoiled.

'I then phoned our insurers and they advised throwing a sweet at someone would be viewed as negligence rather than a simple accident if someone was hurt.

'The audience will still get the sweets because we will have the ushers pass them round and lob them a short distance along rows. They will just not be thrown at force towards the back row from the stage.'

But Helen McDermott – artistic director of the panto hit by the ban, *Babes in the Wood & Robin Hood* – said: 'I think this is just another example of the health and safety culture going mad. Throwing sweets is one of the great traditional parts of pantomimes and children have enjoyed it for years.'

And even a spokesman for the Royal Society for the Prevention of Accidents, said: 'This seems like an overreaction to what ought to be a bit of traditional Christmas fun.'

Yet, sadly, for children off to the Gorleston Pavilion Theatre, Norfolk, some of the fun is now... behind you!

Tesco at Blackpool banned a local band from playing Christmas Carols outside their store. The store said it was because too many shoppers might gather to listen and cause congestion.

Wimborne council in Dorset bans the ancient Christmas tradition of firing muskets into the air as the noise will scare children, according to a *Daily Telegraph* report in November 2008.

Ed Balls makes Christmas safe

Whatever you do this Christmas, don't let children into the kitchen while you are cooking the turkey. Always finish your drink to avoid a youngster having a taste and getting alcohol poisoning. And, of course, never hang baubles on the tree. They might break and give someone a headache. These are among eleven tips issued by Children's Secretary Ed Balls to help make Christmas safe. His department printed 150,000 leaflets with this guidance [from *Daily Mail* December 22 2008].

Killer knives, knuckle-dusters … and tinsel

The *Guardian* reported a new threat to children's lives in a report in December, 2004. 'Headteachers in some inner-city schools have had to introduce initiatives to stop tearaway pupils from bringing knives, knuckle-dusters and other weapons into the classroom.

'But a school on the edge of the Cotswolds has felt the need to go a little further, ordering students not to wear tinsel at a Christmas party for fear they could be throttled.'

It had become customary for some pupils of Chipping Sodbury school to wear tinsel around their necks at a 'mufti' party which they were allowed to attend out of uniform. To the bemusement of parents and children, the school imposed the ban, citing 'health and safety' reasons. The deputy headteacher said they wanted children to have a good time, but if tinsel were worn around the neck it could be pulled tight, 'and we don't want anything like that'.

The tinsel ban might not be as odd as some parents think. The Royal Society for the Prevention of Accidents says around 1,000 people are hurt every Christmas in trimmings-related accidents.

Cathedral puts out Christingle flames

For the first time in more than 250 years, according to the *Daily Telegraph* in December 2006, children will not be allowed to carry candles at a cathedral service in case their hair catches fire.

There is no record of a child going up in flames since the Christingle service began at Chelmsford Cathedral in 1747. But children this year will carry fluorescent glow sticks rather than the traditional candles set in oranges.

Eric Pickles, the MP for nearby Brentwood and Ongar, criticised the move, saying Christmas was becoming homogenised, dull and full of earnestness. 'Eventually, they will work out a way to take all the fun out of Christmas.'

The Christmas Eve service is centred on each child's Christingle – an orange with four spikes in it holding sweets and, usually, a lighted candle in the top, symbolising Christ's light and love.

One of the organisers claimed that some parents were concerned about the safety risk. 'Last Christmas more than 300 youngsters took part in the ceremony and that meant there were too many candles for the organisers to light,' he said. 'Things were so crammed some parents were very worried about candles and chilren's hair.'

Not wanting to be killjoys, the organisers introduced an alternative. Children 'process to the altar where they hand over cardboard tubes with money for the Children's Society. The children then go back to their seats where they are given a Christingle. The idea is that they then form a circle with the candles lit, the lights go down and it looks magical.

'Last year, there were so many you couldn't do this and we had problems getting children back to their seats.' So fluorescent tubes were proposed, though it had not been decided yet when the children would shake them to activate the light. 'We thought we would give it a try ... But if it doesn't work, we will go back to candles. We don't want to spoil things but we also don't want to put anyone in danger.'

Would you believe it

Here's a selection of some of our favourite stories which don't fit into the previous chapter headings.

Books can hurt you

A man who wrote a book about soldiers during the First World War was told he needed an expensive insurance policy if he wanted to sell the book on council premises. The insurance was needed in case anyone dropped a book on their feet or cut their fingers on the paper and tried to sue the council.

Slow down, old man!

[*Daily Telegraph July 28 2008*]

An 80-year-old former Olympian has been banned from running the wrong way up escalators because it is too dangerous.

The runner, who represented Britain at three Olympic Games, was stopped from trying to recreate his old training regime from the 1950s at a department store by the manager. The grandfather-of-five managed to run up the moving stairs in a Surrey department story but was then told he would be banned from Elphicks in Farnham if he tried the stunt again.

Foiled by Elphicks, he turned his attention to other shops for a while but has now decided to hang up his escalator running shoes, saying he had proved what he wanted to.

'I started doing it last month because I was turning 80. I must have done it three or four times. But at the top of the escalator is the women's underwear department, and the woman who runs it told me to stop.'

A spokesman for the store said, 'It is extremely dangerous and we'll get kids doing it if they see him, which is something we want to avoid.'

This next is one of those stories one almost wants to be true, but more likely it's an example of how reports can get out of hand.

Paint your bees

It's about a gardener who wanted to keep bees in his allotment and was told by a council official that he had to PAINT them. Ken J, 37, told the *Sun* newspaper he was told he would have to put a dab of paint on each insect to identify him as the owner if they stung people. He said: 'I was incredulous. I told him there was no way I would paint them all. It's absolute madness.'

But a spokesman for Caerphilly Borough Council insisted the official's remark 'was made in jest, off-the-cuff. He didn't think he would be taken seriously.'

Shock report – passengers don't like being late

A report that took two years to compile and cost taxpayers £500,000, according to *The Week* for May 30 2009, concluded that rail passengers may experience 'negative' feelings if their train is late and no one tells them why. The 178-page report, by the Rail Safety and Standards Board, also found that passengers are likely to be in a 'positive frame of mind' if their train is punctual and announcements are audible.

Candles can create flames

In another attack on cosy Middle England, bureaucrats have told a man who sells honey and 'hive products' that he can sell candles only if he warns customers that there is a risk they might start a fire. The market trader said, 'I was absolutely dumbfounded when I was told I couldn't sell candles because they don't carry a health warning. I thought the whole point of lighting a candle was to have a fire on the top', he added naively.

What to do with a Wellington boot

Would you know what to do if somebody gave you a pair of Wellington boots? Don't worry if you don't, because they now come with a 24-page user's manual. It is printed in ten languages and tells you everything you need to know (and much, much more …) about how to use your new boots. The booklet recommends you try each boot to make sure it fits before you set out on a walk. The manual is necessary to comply with an EU directive for personal protective equipment.

Council had to ask gay men before cutting back bushes

Most visitors to a popular beauty spot would welcome overgrown bushes being cut back, reckoned the *Daily Mail* in July 2008. But, the newspaper reported, a council has to tread carefully after being told that to some members of the gay community, the dense undergrowth was something to be protected.

Removing it would discriminate against the gay men who use the area for outdoor sex, campaigners claimed.

Visitors to the Downs near Bristol's spectacular Avon Gorge have complained about the 'inappropriate sexual activity' which can be punishable by up to six months in prison. Despite this the city council felt obliged to consult gay rights groups about their concerns over its plan to clear away the bushes to improve the scenery and protect rare wildlife.

Walking too slowly
Pensioner to lose his guide dog for walking too slowly

[*Daily Mail August 12 2008*]

For almost 20 years, Eric G has relied on a guide dog to be his eyes and give him independence.

But now the frail widower, who was born blind, has been told he is not eligible for a new guide dog because he walks too slowly.

Officials said the 78-year-old may not receive a replacement when his present dog, Alice, retires as he is in poor health which affects his mobility.

The news has deeply upset the retired factory worker, who has had a guide dog since he was 60. 'I'm not Linford Christie – I am an old man not in the greatest of health. I suffer from sciatica so its hard for me to walk quickly,' he said.

Cooing at new-born babies banned as it breaches their human rights

Calderdale Royal Hospital in Halifax was reported in September 2005 as having banned visitors from cooing at new-born babies following a staff advice session which highlighted the need for respect for the dignity of patients.

Signs have been put up in the hospital saying, 'What makes you think I want to be looked at?' A spokeswoman for Calderdale and Huddersfield NHS Trust said the advice was also to do with reducing infection as well as upholding rights.

However, Debbie Lawson, neo-natal manager at the hospital's special baby care unit, said, 'Cooing should be a thing of the past because these are little people with the same rights as you or me.'

Philip Davies MP, Yorkshire Spokesman for the Campaign Against Political Correctness, whose youngest son was born only a few months ago, said, 'Never mind the asylum, the lunatics have now taken over the maternity ward.' He also added, 'However, I do think that if someone was cooing over a baby and the baby sat up and asked them not to do it because it was infringing their human rights then I think the person should respect the baby's wishes.'

Goggles banned by the goggle police

[*Daily Mail September 19 2008*]

He's been swimming all around the world and never caused a ripple of concern.

But Roland G hadn't reckoned on the goggle police at his local pool. His special mask stops water going up his nose and has a single eye piece which does not press against his face. But now, almost inevitably, it has fallen foul of the 'elf and safety enforcers'.

Their ban on his mask has left Mr G, who has been swimming at a leisure centre in north London for 30 years, high and dry. Pool bosses defended their decision to eject him – declaring his goggles were not shatterproof and breached industry guidelines.

Pupils in Mold, north Wales, have been told [*Press Association June 5 2009*], they can now only wear goggles for swimming on medical grounds. The headteacher is worried that goggles might snap onto a child's face and cause permanent eye injury.

Dead eels killed off

It might not be everyone's idea of fun, but Conger Cuddling – or grown men whacking each other with a five-foot dead eel – has raised thousands of pounds for the Royal National Lifeboat Institution over the past 30 years. Not any more. Sadly, one single protestor claimed it was disrespectful to dead animals and the contest has now been banned.

Pantomime Props

We could hardly believe the story of the village panto group that had to register its wooden swords and plastic guns with the local police, keeping them under lock and key and naming someone responsible for moving the 'weapons' at any time.

A spokesman for the drama group said: 'Our only gun was a panto pistol which produces a flag with the word bang on it. Our local police at Truro were fantastic and they have registered the gun, the two plastic cutlasses and our six wooden swords.'

Prisoners' Legs

[*The Week June 14 2008*]

A security van was sent on a 120-mile round trip to move a prisoner 200 yards between a Crown Court and a Magistrates Court. Police in Northampton claimed that to make the prisoner walk would breach his human rights and endanger public safety, so a van was scrambled from Cambridge 60 miles away, to drive the suspect, who was charged with stealing a cable, down the road.

Car crushed because of open window

A perfectly good car that was taxed, insured and legally parked was reportedly towed away and crushed because the owner had left the windows open half an inch to keep the interior cool. The traffic warden who reported it wasn't concerned that it might be stolen: rather he decided it constituted a fire hazard because lighted matches could have been posted through the windows, and if the car burst into flames it could threaten a nearby electricity substation.

Braille for Air Traffic Controllers
[*Daily Record July 12 2008*]
With the nation's skies becoming ever busier, you'd imagine good eyesight would be essential for anyone wanting to be an air traffic controller.

But not, it seems, on the Isles of Scilly. The islands' St Mary's Airport have just advertised for someone with the skills to direct planes, but are offering potential candidates application packs in Braille, large text or audio format.

And that's despite the job description stating that applicants must be capable of observing weather conditions at the airport.

While the islands' council said the offer was standard procedure, the baffling advertisement is being viewed as just the latest example of political correctness being taken too far.

Traditional fairy tales 'not PC enough'
[*Daily Telegraph January 12 2009*]
In further reports of the threat to children's reading, parents have stopped reading traditional fairytales to their children because they are too scary and not politically correct, according to research.

Favourites such as *Snow White and the Seven Dwarfs*, *Cinderella* and *Rapunzel* are being dropped by some families who fear children are being emotionally damaged.

132

A third of parents refused to read *Little Red Riding Hood* because she walks through woods alone and finds her grandmother eaten by a wolf. One in 10 said *Snow White* should be re-named because 'the dwarf reference is not PC'.

Rapunzel was considered 'too dark' and Cinderella has been dumped amid fears she is treated like a slave and forced to do all the housework.

The poll of 3,000 British parents – taken for thebabywebsite.com – revealed a quarter of mothers now rejected some classic fairy tales.

A mother-of-three from Sevenoaks, Kent, told researchers:'I loved the old fairy stories when I was growing up. I still read my children some of the classics like *Sleeping Beauty* and *Goldilocks*, but I must admit I've not read them *The Gingerbread Man* or *Hansel and Gretel*.

'They are both a bit scary and I remember having difficulty sleeping after being read those ones when I was little.'

Two-thirds of parents said traditional fairy tales had stronger morality messages than many modern children's stories. But many said they were no longer appropriate to soothe youngsters before bed. Almost 20 per cent of adults said they refused to read *Hansel and Gretel* because the children were abandoned in a forest – and it might give their own sons and daughters nightmares. A fifth did not like to read *The Gingerbread Man* as he gets eaten by a fox. The most popular book read at bedtime is now *The Very Hungry Caterpillar* by Eric Carle. The simple tale, which features a greedy caterpillar eating too much food, was written in 1969.

It also emerged 65 per cent of parents preferred to read their children happier tales at bedtime, such as the *Mr Men*, *The Gruffalo* and *Winnie the Pooh*.

Three quarters of mothers and fathers try to avoid stories which might give their children nightmares and half of all parents would not consider reading a single fairy tale to their child until they reached the age of five.

Sniffer dogs to wear 'Muslim' bootees

[*Sunday Times July 2008*]
Police sniffer dogs will have to wear bootees when searching the homes of Muslims so as not to cause offence.

Guidelines being drawn up by the Association of Chief Police Officers (Acpo) urge awareness of religious sensitivities when using dogs to search for drugs and explosives. The guidelines, to be published this year, were designed to cover mosques but have been extended to include other buildings.

Where Muslims object, officers will be obliged to use sniffer dogs only in exceptional cases. Where dogs are used, they will have to wear bootees with rubber soles. 'We are trying to ensure that police forces are aware of sensitivities that people can have with the dogs to make sure they are not going against any religious or cultural element within people's homes. It is being addressed and forces are working towards doing it,' Acpo said.

Problems faced by the use of sniffer dogs were highlighted last week when Tayside police were forced to apologise for a crime prevention poster featuring a German Shepherd puppy, in response to a complaint by a Muslim councillor. Islamic injunctions warn Muslims against contact with dogs, which are regarded as 'unclean'.

Police dogs at present are issued with footwear only at scenes of explosions to prevent them injuring their paws on broken glass.

One of Britain's leading imams said the measures were unnecessary: 'In Islamic law the dog is not regarded as impure, only its saliva is. Most Islamic schools of law agree on that. If security measures require to send a dog into a house, then it has to be done. I think Acpo needs to consult better and more widely.

'I know in the Muslim community there is a hang-up against dogs, but this is cultural. Also, we know the British like dogs; we Muslims should do our bit to change our attitudes.'

Bible moved to top shelf in libraries over inequality fears

Librarians have been told to move the Koran and Bible to their top shelves to avoid offending the Islamic community, according to a recent *Daily Telegraph* report.

Muslims complained that the Koran is often displayed on the lower shelves, which is deemed offensive as many believe the holy book should be placed above 'commonplace things'.

As a result, library officials were told to keep all holy books, including the Bible, on their top shelves in the interests of equality.

The move has caused concern among Christian charities that the Bible will be out of many people's reach and sight.

The situation came to light in guidance published by the Museums, Libraries and Archives Council, a quango answering to the Culture Secretary on how to handle controversial materials.

Pointless Jobs

Councils have been accused of wasting millions of pounds of public money on pointless jobs, including a £23,000 composting supervisor and a toothbrush advisor for infants.

Such roles, often the product of 'political correctness' or the burgeoning health and safety culture, form part of a public sector that is expanding despite the downturn which has seen private workers face redundancies and pay freezes.

'There has been a huge boom in the number of unnecessary and bizarre jobs in local government in recent years,' said Matthew Elliot, chief executive of the Taxpayers' Alliance, a pressure group.

Many positions in local government have their origins in health and safety regulations. Tewkesbury Council, Gloucestershire, deemed it necessary to appoint a 'falls prevention fitness adviser', primarily to help elderly people.

In Scotland, Angus Council employs a 'bouncy castle attendant' on £13,000 a year while Falkirk pays a part time 'toothbrush assistant' £3,000 a year to teach nursery children how to clean their teeth. The same council also employs a 'cheerleading development officer'.

No 'blacking up' in new Al Jolson musical

[Daily Telegraph February 18 2009]

The producers of a new musical about the Broadway star Al Jolson have been criticised for deciding that the actor who plays him will not wear his trademark 'black face' during the show.

The American singer and actor, who became the star of the first 'talking picture' was famous for performing in black make-up in the 1920s – a style later copied in the 'Black and White Minstrel Show'.

But the producers of *Jolson & Co*, which opens in Edinburgh next week ahead of a UK tour, have dropped the scene in which the lead traditionally sings 'My Mammy' while wearing make-up in order to avoid 'causing offence'.

Michael Harrison, the producer, said blacking up was 'historically correct' but added: 'In this day and age we are not out to offend anyone. There is reference to blacking up in the script but we didn't feel it was necessary to include it in the show.'

The decision was taken despite the fact that Equity, the actors' union, said that a Jolson show was one of the very few occasions on which it 'might not actively object because it was about a white artist who blacked up'.

Laura Midgley of the Campaign Against Political Correctness said the decision made 'absolutely no sense' and was a clumsy case of 'political correctness taking the place of authenticity.' She added that when a councillor in London was criticised for blacking up for a fancy dress party, it was Nelson Mandela who came to his aid saying,

'We should not read racism into actions that are clearly innocent.'

Allan Stewart, who takes on the lead role, appeared in a different London musical about Jolson 12 years ago that did include a 'blackface' number and did not cause an outcry. He said he believed the blacked-up number should be in the show, but added that 'even the slightest sign of negativity' could be bad news for the production.

Richard Holloway, the former Episcopal Bishop of Edinburgh, said it was a difficult call, adding: 'In a sense to be authentic about Jolson, that's what he did.

'On the other hand, it always was offensive, but I don't know how you would get round that. I remember as a kid I used to enjoy them, I went to all the movies. One thought nothing of it, but it is terribly demeaning.'

Jay Berkow, the American co-writer of the original play, said that its original production in New York included a short black-face sequence. He added: 'It occurs directly after his marriage to Ruby Keeler (the film actress) falls apart and he hides his pain behind the "mask" as he sings the signature song "Mammy".'

Jolson, who died in 1950, was the first recording artist to sell over one million records and was the star of a string of New York shows and in 1927 featured in *The Jazz Singer*, the first 'talking picture'.

The 'Black and White Minstrel Show' later featured songs popularised by Jolson and other vaudeville stars and ran on British television until 1978. The singer is credited with fighting racism on Broadway at the height of his career.

Chaplain at Sandhurst military academy bans the Creed 'so services won't offend minority religions'

[Daily Mail January 31 2009]

Sandhurst Military Academy has dropped the Church of England creed from services over fears that it may offend religious minorities.

The move has outraged worshippers who say centuries of religious tradition have been sacrificed for the sake of political correctness.

Senior chaplain Reverend Jonathan Gough dropped the Christian declaration of faith in God, Father, Son and Holy Spirit, when he took office earlier this month.

Mr Gough – nicknamed the 'Right on Rev' by some of his flock – says he wants to avoid offending non-believers.

Lord Protect us!

[Mail on Sunday August 10 2008]

It's enough to try the patience of a saint.

For centuries the word of God has been preached unhindered from the pulpit in the Church of All Saints – then along came the health and safety jobsworths.

Now the church has been forced to draw up guidelines after being warned by council officials that the pulpit is 'dangerous' and that preachers might be injured while climbing its seven spiral stone steps.

The church in the Wyke Regis area of Weymouth, Dorset, dates from 1172 and has no record of injured clergy.

But health and safety officers suggested the addition of an unsightly handrail to the sixteenth-century pulpit.

Circus clown banned from wearing floppy shoes

[*Daily Mail April 23 2009*]

A Russian performing artist was left genuinely crying the tears of a clown after being told he could no longer wear his giant comedy shoes because they were a health risk.

The clown was performing in Britain with the Moscow State Circus when, while wearing the shoes, he fell from a 10ft-high wire, hurting his left foot. He continued with the show but when he went to hospital later that evening he was told he had broken his metatarsal bone. After a week's recovery he returned to the circus only to be told that his size-18 shoes compromised his health and safety and would have to go.

In his routine, the agile clown dresses himself first while walking on a wire, then within a hoop of fire, and plays a drum-kit, trumpet and double-bass all at the same time.

The 40-year-old, from Temruk, in Russia told the *Daily Mail*: 'The shoes are an important part of my costume, and I was disappointed to be told I couldn't do this part of my act.

'Now I've got to do the balancing act in normal-sized shoes and it just won't be the same.'

The general manager for the circus, agreed, saying: 'I think it will definitely detract from the visual aspect of the performance.

'It's very important because there's a language barrier to the whole performance, as it's in Russian. Plus these clowns don't look like the usual clowns we think of – they have minimal face paint and aren't as garish, so it's important for them to wear the shoes.

'But we live in a litigation world, and I guess we just have to follow through these procedures. It's a real balancing act.'

The health and safety adviser to the circus, said he wasn't a fan of political correctness. 'The problem is he (the clown) can't feel the wire between his feet with the boots on,' he said.

Slippers are not for slipping

If you believe the statistics, then the most dangerous place in the world is actually your own home. Sadly that reassuring, warm, safe feeling we all get when we're nicely inside our own four walls is actually lulling us into a state of false security. You and I are more likely to have an accident, or even die, at home than anywhere else.

Fortunately, few people can be bothered to legislate against such accidents, as we are unlikely to launch compensation claims against ourselves, or indeed our loved ones. This means we're at liberty to act as recklessly as we like once we've shut the front door: we can light fires, climb loft ladders, prepare food and wear slippers to our hearts' content without even the bother of carrying out a risk assessment.

A slippers amnesty has been announced with old people urged to hand in worn-out and potentially dangerous footwear, according to a *Daily Telegraph* report in December, 2007. In exchange, the charity Age Concern will be handing out 1,000 new pairs of slippers in a bid to cut down on accidents in the home.

The Hampshire branch of the charity is holding a series of 'slipper roadshows' around the county after national figures showed that one third of the 370,000 falls suffered by the over-65s at home are caused by worn out slippers.

John Morton, assistant director of Hampshire Age Concern, said trained experts would be on hand to give advice on slipper fit and selection. Indoor footwear would be available in a range of sizes and colours for ladies and gentlemen on a first come, first serviced basis, for free, to older residents only.

Mr Morton said: 'Many people may not replace their slippers because they are comfortable. But they may not realise the importance of slippers that fit well. They are like other dangers such as loose carpets.'

Roger Vincent, a spokesman for the Royal Society for the Prevention of Accidents, said: 'A slipper trip or fall is the most likely accident that people of a certain age will have.

'Slippers are the kind of items that people tend to keep for a long time so the soles might not grip as well and the fabric might not provide as much support. People are loath to throw them away because they are comfortable.

'But a worn-down slipper is a potentially dangerous item – it will not protect your feet and will not keep you stable as you walk along. A slipper amnesty may sound odd but it is a great thing.'

Health and safety hit back

With so many mind-boggling genuine health and safety stories going around, it's small wonder that some are exaggerated and distorted, and others are complete fabrications. It's very hard to tell which are factual, and which aren't.

The Health and Safety Executive, with 3,500 staff in 28 offices around the country, is so fed up with being asked to comment on fictional tales, that it has dedicated a website to identify false stories, with a special 'myth of the month' slot. You can find it at: www.hse.gov.uk/myth/. This is well worth a visit for a chuckle at the banal guidelines and advice HSE offer, almost as amusing as the myths they seek to debunk.

So fed up, too, that chairman (sorry, chairwoman) Judith Hackitt gave an interview with *The Times* in April 2009 to explain the difference between Health & Safety (definitely OK) and lower-case health and safety (often a bit daft). But she admits that the H & S Executive haven't always got it right. There is the little matter of courses to teach people how to use ladders – 'I really don't understand why we have to tell people, but sadly we do.' Another cause célèbre is the H & S guidelines on wobbly gravestones, and the estimated £2.5 million local councils have been paying out to employ certified 'topple-testers' who use a special German-built machine to test the stability of gravestones. More recently, the Executive has been getting stick from the media over their Brussels-inspired regulations to set a maximum workplace noise level. This has led some musicians to wear ear-plugs. On a BBC *Panorama* programme around this time, some complained this meant they could play Mozart but not Mahler. 'It's a real problem,' Judith Hackitt told Hugo Rifkind, 'some musicians do suffer noise-induced hearing loss through sustained exposure to music. It's not the rules and the guidance we put out that brings out the 'Health and Safety gone mad' stories. It's more often local authorities or businesses being afraid of legal action. When I trip over a paving stone in the street, I'll look for someone else to blame.' She's absolutely right about the compensation culture, of course.

In some cases the line between truth and fiction is blurred by the media's enthusiasm for printing the kind of news that makes us shake our collective heads, raise our eyebrows and wonder what the world is coming to. It's not all their fault. There's usually a reason why these false stories make the press.

For example, the HSE cites one puppeteer who was sent a letter by an event organiser asking him to carry out a risk assessment before setting out his stall. There was a huge tabloid hoo-ha over this; in fact, when the puppeteer asked why an assessment was necessary, the organiser backed off. In response Glyn Edwards, puppeteer and former producer of children's television show 'Tiswas' has added a new character to his Punch and Judy show – the Health and Safety Inspector. He intervenes when the crocodile makes an appearance, and also has something to say about the unhygienic way the string of sausages is bandied around. That's the way to do it!

Another example of a myth is the story about firefighters' poles being banned for Health and Safety reasons.

The *Daily Telegraph* in particular got a little hot under the collar, saying that a new £2.4 million fire station had been built without a pole because of 'fears that firefighters could sprain their ankles as they hit the ground.'

The paper quoted the station officer as saying: 'It takes about a second and a half to slide down the pole, as opposed to 15 or 20 seconds to run down two flights of stairs. Seconds can be critical when responding to a 999 call.

'In more than 30 years I have seen one or two accidents with poles, compared with tens of accidents with people tripping on stairs while responding to incidents.'

It does sound ludicrous, but the HSE insists this was nothing to do with them, the design of the new building simply didn't incorporate the traditional method of getting from one floor to another because of space constraints. Shame...

The authors of this book were also disappointed to discover that the 'hard hats for trapeze artists' story isn't true, given that it received acres of coverage in the national press, and continues to be mooted as a fine example of bureaucratic idiocy.

'This story is utter nonsense,' says the HSE unequivocally. 'There never were any such regulations.'

It also denies the annual 'killjoy' accusations that come flying its way every Christmas, when workers the length and breadth of the country are allegedly banned from putting up Christmas decorations.

Not so, says the HSE. It just wants people to put up their decoration sensibly, ie: not attempting to balance on wheelie chairs while sticking up the tinsel.

You have to feel sympathy for the people who work in Health and Safety, and who are so regularly mocked, when all they're trying to do is prevent injury. It's the people who profit from the compensation culture who are the real baddies! So we take off our safety hats and raise them to the HSE for putting up the website and doing its bit to fight back.

'The health and safety culture is a tyranny our nation can ill afford'

The backlash against the 'health and safety' culture is now assuming political proportions, with Tory leader David Cameron jumping on the bandwagon. The passage in his speech to party faithful in Birmingham last autumn won him one of the longest rounds of applause, according to the *Daily Express.*

Commenting on the ongoing nonsense about conkers, the paper said in May, 2009: 'The reason we have over-zealous teachers, many of whom have banned conkers altogether, is that the Government has created an atmosphere of fear in which teachers feel they can no longer use their commonsense.

'It [the Government] has championed lawyers' no win/no fee agreements which have led to an explosion in 'claims factories', which send canvassers on to the streets to fish for passers-by who have had an accident at work, school or anywhere else.

'No wonder, when faced with a barrage of claims, public servants and businesses have been driven to take the safe option and ban anything that could be construed as risky. Not only that, schools, hospitals and the like have been besieged with inspectors. Government campaigns have fed paranoia over paedophiles, which has wrought havoc in schools, swimming pools and other public places.

'As David Cameron alluded to in his speech, state schools are now forbidden from organising French exchanges unless all parents involved have had an enhanced criminal

148

records check. As a result, many schools have opted to throw in the towel and end their exchange programmes after generations, in spite of there not being a single recorded case of a pupil abused by an exchange family.

'The Health and Safety Executive (HSE), a government quango, protested at Mr Cameron's assertion that teachers are no longer allowed to stick plasters on pupils' cuts. Technically, the HSE is correct: there is no law banning plasters in schools. What it doesn't admit, however, is that the obsession with child abuse has reached such heights that many teachers, directed by education authorities, feel they have no option but to cease all physical contact with pupils.'

STOP PRESS

And still they pour in. These last 'health and safety' and political correctness stories came to light as we were going to press.

These clothes are not for dying in

Grieving families in Yorkshire are being urged to dress their loved ones in 'eco-shrouds' for cremation, as clothes emit too much pollution. Crematoria in the Kirklees area have banned families from dressing the dead in their own clothes, telling them they must pay £60 for a council-approved shroud.

Jazzing up the church

A series of proposals for jazzing up Church of England services has been published as part of its Fresh Expressions programme, which aims to attract the young to the church. These include reciting psalms in 'beat poetry' style, to the accompaniment of African drums; saying prayers for the head of Google, and performing 'U2charists', in which the congregation sings U2 songs instead of hymns.

Too bad you've lost your cat

A pensioner was threatened with a £75 fine for putting up posters of her missing cat.

When Mrs S, 63, received a phone call in response she thought it would be to give her the news that her beloved Siamese cat had been found.

But the caller said he was from the council and that he would send someone round to enforce the fine for flyposting if Mrs S did not take down the posters. The pensioner, from Worthing, West Sussex, was left so upset by the call that she has taken down most of the posters – reducing the chances of finding her cat.

The call from Worthing Borough Council came after Mrs Sears stuck about 20 posters on to nearby phone boxes, trees and lamp-posts. A council spokesman said, 'Our employee wasn't seeking to be a jobsworth but just to ask her to reduce the number of posters she has displayed in the area'.

And finally, spotted in a National Trust garden in Cornwall – a notice warning visitors that insects including bees and wasps can sting.

All very amusing, but is it not time something was done to curb this sort of nonsense? The courts could start by being more severe on spurious compensation claims — we suspect some judges are already tightening up — and steps could be taken to limit the activities of parasitical 'no win, no fee' operators.

Remember, it's a dangerous world out there but according to some statistics it's even more dangerous to stay at home.